T0040424

# THOMAS KINSELLA

# SELECTED POEMS

# THOMAS KINSELLA

# SELECTED POEMS

WAKE FOREST UNIVERSITY PRESS

First North American edition published 2010

Copyright © 2010 by Thomas Kinsella
All rights reserved

For permission to reproduce or
broadcast these poems, write to
Wake Forest University Press
Post Office Box 7333
Winston-Salem, NC 27109
www.wfu.edu/wfupress

Typeset by XL Publishing Services, Tiverton
Printed on acid-free, recycled paper
in the United States of American

LCCN 2010922056
ISBN 978-1-930630-40-6

First published in Great Britain in 2007
by Carcanet Press Limited

# Contents

## from *Poems* (1956)

## from *Another September* (1958)

## from *Moralities* (1960)

## from *Downstream* (1962)

## from *Wormwood* (1966)

## from *Nightwalker and Other Poems* (1968)

## from *New Poems* (1973)

# PEPPERCANISTER POEMS

## *A Selected Life* (1972)

## *Vertical Man* (1973)

## from *One* (1974)

## from *A Technical Supplement* (1976)

## from *Song of the Night and Other Poems* (1978)

## from *Songs of the Psyche* (1985)

## from *Out of Ireland* (1987)

## from *Personal Places* (1990)

## from *Poems from Centre City* (1990)

# from *Madonna and Other Poems* (1991)

# from *The Familiar* (1999)

# from *Godhead* (1999)

# from *Citizen of the World* (2000)

# from *Littlebody* (2000)

# from *Marginal Economy* (2006)

from

# Poems

(1956)

## Night Songs

### 1

Now, as I sink in sleep,
My heart is cut down,
Nothing – poetry nor love –
Achieving.

\*

Turns again in my room,
The crippled leopard.
Paw-pad, configured
Yellow light of his eyes,
Pass, repass, repass.

Quiet, my hand; he is tame.

Soon, while I dream, will step
And stir the sunken dawn.

Before I woke there entered in
A woman with a golden skin
    That tangled with the light.
A tang of orchards climbed the stair
And dwindled in the waxen air,
    Crisping the midnight,
And the white pillows of my bed
On apple-tasted darkness fed.
    Weakened with appetite
Sleep broke like a dish wherein
A woman lay with golden skin.

## *Midsummer*

Hereabouts the signs are good.
Propitious creatures of the wood
    After their fashion
Have pitied and blessed before our eyes.
All unpremeditated lies
    Our scattered passion.

Flowers whose name I do not know
Make happy signals to us. O
    Did ever bees
Stumble on such a quiet before!
The evening is a huge closed door
    And no one sees

How we, absorbed in our own art,
Have locked ourselves inside one heart,
    Grown silent and,
Under beech and sacred larch,
Watched as though it were an arch
    That heart expand.

Something that for this long year
Had hid and halted like a deer
Turned marvellous,
Parted the tragic grasses, tame,
Lifted its perfect head and came
To welcome us.

We have, dear reason, of this glade
An endless tabernacle made,
An origin.
Well for whatever lonely one
Will find this right place to lay down
His desert in.


## Soft, to your Places

Soft, to your places, animals.
Your legendary duty calls.
It is, to be
Lucky for my love and me
*And yet we have seen that all's*
*A fiction that is heard of love's difficulty.*

And what if the simple primrose show
That mighty work went on below
Before it grew
A moral miracle for us two?
*Since of ourselves we know*
*Beauty to be an easy thing, this will do.*

But O when beauty's brought to pass
Will Time set down his hour-glass
And rest content,
His hand upon that monument?
*Unless it is so, alas*
*That the heart's calling is but to go naked and diffident.*

Soft, to your places, love; I kiss
Because it is, because it is.

# A Lady of Quality

In hospital where windows meet
With sunlight in a pleasing feat
    Of airy architecture
My love has sweets and grapes to eat,
The air is like a laundered sheet,
    The world's a varnished picture.

Books and flowers at her head
Make living-quarters of her bed
    And give a certain style
To our pillow-chat, the nonsense said
To bless the room from present dread
    Just for a brittle while.

For obvious reasons we ignore
The leaping season out-of-door,
    Light lively as a ferret,
Woodland walks, a crocused shore,
The transcendental birds that soar
    And tumble in high spirit

While under this hygienic ceiling
Where my love lies down for healing
    Tiny terrors grow,
Reflected in a look, revealing
That her care is spent concealing
    What, perhaps, I know.

'Ended and done with' never ceases,
Constantly the heart releases
    Wild geese to the past.
Look, how they circle poignant places,
Falling to sorrow's fowling-pieces
    With soft plumage aghast.

We may regret, and must abide.
Grief, the hunter's, fatal stride
	Among the darkening hearts
Has gone too long on either side.
Our trophied love must now divide
	Into its separate parts

And you go down with womankind
Who in her beauty has combined
	And focused human hungers,
With country ladies who could wind
A nation's love-affair with mind
	Around their little fingers,

While I communicate again
Recovered order to my pen
	To find a further answer
As, having looked all night in vain,
A weary prince will sigh and then
	Take a familiar dancer.

Now the window's turning dark
And ragged rooks across the Park
	Mix with branches; all
The clocks about the building mark
The hour. The random is at work
	Between us: two petals fall.

A train lifts up a lonely cry ...
Our fingertips together lie
	Upon the counterpane.
It will be hard, it seems, and I
Would wish my heart to justify
	What qualities remain.

from

# Another September

(1958)

## In the Ringwood

As I roved out impatiently
Good Friday with my bride
To drink in the rivered Ringwood
The draughty season's pride
A fell dismay held suddenly
Our feet on the green hill-side.

The yellow Spring on Vinegar Hill,
The smile of Slaney water,
The wind that swept the Ringwood,
Grew dark with ancient slaughter.
My love cried out and I beheld her
Change to Sorrow's daughter.

'Ravenhair, what rending
Set those red lips a-shriek,
And dealt those locks in black lament
Like blows on your white cheek,
That in your looks outlandishly
Both woe and fury speak?'

As sharp a lance as the fatal heron
There on the sunken tree
Will strike in the stones of the river
Was the gaze she bent on me.
Oh her robe into her right hand
She gathered grievously.

'Many times the civil lover
Climbed that pleasant place,
Many times despairing
Died in his love's face,
His spittle turned to vinegar,
Blood in his embrace.

Love that is every miracle
Is torn apart and rent.
The human turns awry
The poles of the firmament.
The fish's bright side is pierced
And good again is spent.

Though every stem on Vinegar Hill
And stone on the Slaney's bed
And every leaf in the living Ringwood
Builds till it is dead
Yet heart and hand, accomplished,
Destroy until they dread.

Dread, a grey devourer,
Stalks in the shade of love.
The dark that dogs our feet
Eats what is sickened of.
The End that stalks Beginning
Hurries home its drove.'

I kissed three times her shivering lips.
I drank their naked chill.
I watched the river shining
Where the heron wiped his bill.
I took my love in my icy arms
In the Spring on Ringwood Hill.

# Another September

Dreams fled away, this country bedroom, raw
With the touch of the dawn, wrapped in a minor peace,
Hears through an open window the garden draw
Long pitch black breaths, lay bare its apple trees,
Ripe pear trees, brambles, windfall-sweetened soil,
Exhale rough sweetness against the starry slates.
Nearer the river sleeps St John's, all toil
Locked fast inside a dream with iron gates.

Domestic Autumn, like an animal
Long used to handling by those countrymen,
Rubs her kind hide against the bedroom wall
Sensing a fragrant child come back again
– Not this half-tolerated consciousness
That plants its grammar in her yielding weather
But that unspeaking daughter, growing less
Familiar where we fell asleep together.

Wakeful moth-wings blunder near a chair,
Toss their light shell at the glass, and go
To inhabit the living starlight. Stranded hair
Stirs on the still linen. It is as though
The black breathing that billows her sleep, her name,
Drugged under judgement, waned and – bearing daggers
And balances – down the lampless darkness they came,
Moving like women: Justice, Truth, such figures.

# Clarence Mangan

Sometimes, charting the heroes and animals of night-time,
Sudden unhappinesses would bewilder me,
Strayed in the long void of youth
Where nothing is understood.

Later, all mankind calling,
I, being anxious, eager to please, shouted my fear
That something was wrong.

Back to a wall, facing tumultuous talking faces,
Once I lost the reason for speech. My heart was taken,
Stretched with terror by only a word a mouth had uttered.

Long I waited to know what naked meeting
Would come with what was moving behind my eyes
And desolating what I touched.

Over a glass, or caught in lamplight,
Caught on the edge of act, my hand
Is suddenly stopped and fills with waiting.

Out of the shadows behind my laughter
Surgical fingers come
And I am strapped to a table.

Pitiless, again I ply the knife.

# The Monk

He tramped in the fading light
Of a late February day
Between hedges stiff with the wind.

His boots trod stone and clay.
His blown habit swung
In the wet daylight's decay.

A spade across his shoulder
Slanted into the sky.
Sunk in the cowl his quiet eye.

A sense of scrubbed flesh in the path;
A thought of washing in cold hours
When dreams are scrubbed off

In a chill room, huge flowers,
Night blooms, accidentally plucked,
Each dawn devours;

Of a haggard taste in the mouth
Savouring in death a tide of light,
Spring in February night.

# Baggot Street Deserta

Lulled, at silence, the spent attack.
The will to work is laid aside.
The breaking-cry, the strain of the rack,
Yield, are at peace. The window is wide
On a crawling arch of stars, and the night
Reacts faintly to the mathematic
Passion of a cello suite
Plotting the quiet of my attic.
A mile away the river toils
Its buttressed fathoms out to sea;
Tucked in the mountains, many miles
Away from its roaring outcome, a shy
Gasp of waters in the gorse
Is sonneting origins. Dreamers' heads
Lie mesmerised in Dublin's beds
Flashing with images, Adam's morse.

A cigarette, the moon, a sigh
Of educated boredom, greet
A curlew's lingering threadbare cry
Of common loss. Compassionate,
I add my call of exile, half-
Buried longing, half-serious
Anger and the rueful laugh.
We fly into our risk, the spurious.

Versing, like an exile, makes
A virtuoso of the heart,
Interpreting the old mistakes
And discords in a work of Art
For the One, a private masterpiece
Of doctored recollections. Truth
Concedes, before the dew, its place
In the spray of dried forgettings Youth
Collected when they were a single
Furious undissected bloom.
A voice clarifies when the tingle
Dies out of the nerves of time:
*Endure and let the present punish.*

Looking backward, all is lost;
The Past becomes a fairy bog
Alive with fancies, double crossed
By pad of owl and hoot of dog,
Where shaven, serious-minded men
Appear with lucid theses, after
Which they don the mists again
With trackless, cotton-silly laughter;
Secretly a swollen Burke
Assists a decomposing Hare
To cart a body of good work
With midnight mutterings off somewhere;
The goddess who had light for thighs
Grows feet of dung and takes to bed,
Affronting horror-stricken eyes,
The marsh bird that children dread.

I nonetheless inflict, endure,
Tedium, intracordal hurt,
The sting of memory's quick, the drear
Uprooting, burying, prising apart
Of loves a strident adolescent
Spent in doubt and vanity.
All feed a single stream, impassioned
Now with obsessed honesty,
A tugging scruple that can keep
Clear eyes staring down the mile,
The thousand fathoms, into sleep.

Fingers cold against the sill
Feel, below the stress of flight,
The slow implosion of my pulse
In a wrist with poet's cramp, a tight
Beat tapping out endless calls
Into the dark, as the alien
Garrison in my own blood
Keeps constant contact with the main
Mystery, not to be understood.
Out where imagination arches
Chilly points of light transact
The business of the border-marches

Of the Real, and I – a fact
That may be countered or may not –
Find their privacy complete.

My quarter-inch of cigarette
Goes flaring down to Baggot Street.


# King John's Castle

Not an epic, being not loosely architectured,
    But with epic force, setting the head spinning
With the taut flight earthward of its bulk, King John's
    Castle rams fast down the county of Meath.
This in its heavy ruin. New, a brute bright plateau,
    It held speechless under its cold a whole province of Meath.

Now the man-rot of passages and broken window-casements,
    Vertical drops chuting through three storeys of masonry,
Draughty spiral stairways decaying in the depths,
    Are a labyrinth in the medieval dark. Intriguers
Who prowled here once, into the waiting arms
    Of their own monster, revisit the blowing dust.

Life, a vestigial chill, sighs along the tunnels
    Through the stone face. The great collapsed rooms, the mind
Of the huge head, are dead. Views open inward
    On empty silence; a chapel-shelf, moss-grown, unreachable.
King John directs at the river a grey stare, who once
    Viewed the land in a spirit of moderation and massacre.

Contemplatives, tiny as mice moving over the green
    Mounds below, might take pleasure in the well
Of quiet there, the dark foundations near at hand.
    Up here where the winds weeps bleakly, as though in remembrance
Against our own tombstones, the brave and great might gather.
    For the rest, this is not their fortress.

# Thinking of Mr D.

A man still light of foot, but ageing, took
An hour to drink his glass, his quiet tongue
Danced to such cheerful slander.

He sipped and swallowed with a scathing smile,
Tapping a polished toe.
His sober nod withheld assent.

When he died I saw him twice.
Once as he used retire
On one last murmured stabbing little tale
From the right company, tucking in his scarf.

And once down by the river, under wharf-
Lamps that plunged him in and out of light,
A priestlike figure turning, wolfish-slim,
Quickly aside from pain, in a bodily plight,
To note the oiled reflections chime and swim.

# *Moralities*

## (1960)

## *Moralities*

Bronze entrance doors alive with angels' wings
Mellow the Western face – a field of stone
Furrowed with devils. Saints in martyred rings
Halo vast windows, light as thistledown.
The wagon empties and a hooting clown
Skips up the shallow steps: 'Ho! Feast your eyes!'
Flounced, scalloped, stuffed with hay, gay skin and bone,
Faith, Love, Death, Song, creep after him like flies.

# Faith

## An Old Atheist Pauses by the Sea

I choose at random, knowing less and less.
The shambles of the seashore at my feet
Yield a weathered spiral: I confess
– Appalled at how the waves have polished it –
I know that shores are eaten, rocks are split,
Shells ghosted. Something hates unevenness.
The skin turns porcelain, the nerves retreat,
And then the will, and then the consciousness.

## Into Thy Hands

Diver, noting lightly how the board
Gives to the body, now with like intent
I watch the body give to the instant, seeing
In risk a salty joy: let accident
Complete our dreadful journey into being.

Here possessed of time and flesh at last,
I hurl the Present bodily at the Past.

Outstretched, into the azure chasm he soared.

## A Pillar of the Community

Descending on Merchants' Alley, Lucifer
Gave jet-black evidence of fatherhood.
A column rose to meet him from the mud;
He perched and turned to metal. Polished, foursquare,
A noble savage stopped in stride, he stood.
Now gingerly our honest deals are done
Under that puckish rump, inscribed: Do good.
Some care and a simple faith will get you on.

# Love

## Sisters

Grim Deirdre sought the stony fist, her grief
Capped at last by insult. Pierce's bride,
Sybil Ferriter, fluttered like a leaf
And fell in courtly love to stain the tide.
Each for a murdered husband – hanged in silk
Or speared in harness – threw her body wide,
And offered treachery a bloody milk.
Each cast the other's shadow when she died.

## A Garden on the Point

Now it is Easter and the speckled bean
Breaks open underground, the liquid snail
Winces and waits, trapped on the lawn's light green;
The burdened clothes-line heaves and barks in the gale,
And lost in flowers near the garage wall
Child and mother fumble, tidy, restrain.

And now great ebb tides lift to the light of day
The sea-bed's briny chambers of decay.

# Interlude: Time's Mischief

Love's doubts enrich my words; I stroke them out.
To each felicity, once. He must progress
Who fabricates a path, though all about
Death, Woman, Spring, repeat their first success.

# from *Death*

## The Doldrums

Two months of blood-summer were in store,
Of strike and rising temper, and the thick sun
A sore that never healed; two months more.
Exhaustion settled over sea and land.

We ushered in midnight at Sutton station,
With the towels damp and sandy, loose in the hand.
Our train clove the serene stars with a roar
In peace and power, on the moment planned.

## Dead on Arrival

It smelled our laughter, then, in vivid shroud,
Loomed with averted face (*Dont think, dont think*),
Limped with its poison through the noisy crowd
And chose my glass. It moaned and begged me: 'Drink.'

I woke in mortal terror, every vein
A-flood with my destroyer; then fought free.
I lie in darkness, treasuring in my brain
The full infection, Night's carnality.

# Song

### Handclasp at Euston

The engine screams and Murphy, isolate
– Chalk-white, comedian – in the smoky glare,
Dwindles among the churns and tenders. Weight,
Person, race, the human, dwindle there.
I bow to the cases cluttering the rack,
Their handles black with sweat of exile. Wales,
Wave and home; I close my eyes. The track
Swerves to a greener world: sea-rock, thigh-scales.

### At the Heart

Heraldic, hatched in gold, a sacred tree
Stands absorbed, tinkering with the slight
Thrumming of birds, the flicker of energy
Thrown and caught, the blows and burdens of flight.
Roots deepen; disciplines proliferate
And wings more fragile are brought into play.
Timber matures, the game grows nobler, yet
Not one has sped direct as appetite.

### Fire and Ice

Two creatures face each other, fixed in song,
Satyr and nymph, across the darkening brain.
I dream of reason and the first grows strong,
Drunk as a whirlwind on the sweating grain.
I dream of drunkenness and, freed from strain,
The second murmurs like a fingered gong.
I sink beneath the dream: his words grow sane,
Her pupils glow with pleasure all night long.

from

# *Downstream*

(1962)

I wonder whether one expects
Flowing tie or expert sex
Or even absent-mindedness
Of poets any longer. Less
Candour than the average,
Less confidence, a ready rage,
Alertness when it comes to beer,
An affectation that their ear
For music is a little weak,
These are the attributes we seek;
But surely not the morning train,
The office lunch, the look of pain
Down the blotched suburban grass,
Not the weekly trance at Mass...
Drawing on my sober dress
These, alas, I must confess.

I pat my wallet pocket, thinking
I can spare an evening drinking;
Humming as I catch the bus
Something by Sibelius,
Suddenly – or as I lend
A hand about the house, or bend
Low above an onion bed –
Memory stumbles in the head;
The sunlight flickers once upon
The massive shafts of Babylon
And ragged phrases in a flock
Settle softly, shock by shock.

*And so my bored menagerie*
*Once more emerges: Energy,*
*Blinking, only half awake,*
*Gives its tiny frame a shake;*
*Fouling itself, a giantess,*
*The bloodshot bulk of Laziness*
*Obscures the vision; Discipline*
*Limps after them with jutting chin,*
*Bleeding badly from the calf;*
*Old Jaws-of-Death gives laugh for laugh*
*With Error as they amble past;*
*And there as usual, lying last,*
*Helped along by blind Routine,*
*Futility flogs a tambourine...*

## The Laundress

Her chair drawn to the door,
A basket at her feet,
She sat against the sun
And stitched a linen sheet.
Over harrowed Flanders
August moved the wheat.

Poplars sharing the wind
With Saxony and France
Dreamed at her gate,
Soared in a Summer trance.
A cluck in the cobbled yard:
A shadow changed its stance.

As a fish disturbs the pond
And sinks without a stain
The heels of ripeness fluttered
Under her apron. Then
Her heart grew strained and light
As the shell that shields the grain.

Bluntly through the doorway
She stared at shed and farm,
At yellow fields unstitching
About the hoarded germ,
At land that would spread white
When she had reached her term.

The sower plumps his acre,
Flanders turns to the heat,
The winds of Heaven winnow
And the wheels grind the wheat.
She searched in her basket
And fixed her ruffled sheet.

## Dick King

In your ghost, Dick King, in your phantom vowels I read
That death roves our memories igniting
Love. Kind plague, low voice in a stubbled throat,
You haunt with the taint of age and of vanished good,
Fouling my thought with losses.

Clearly now I remember rain on the cobbles,
Ripples in the iron trough, and the horses' dipped
Faces under the Fountain in James's Street,
When I sheltered my nine years against your buttons
And your own dread years were to come:

And your voice, in a pause of softness, named the dead,
Hushed as though the city had died by fire,
Bemused, discovering…discovering
A gate to enter temperate ghosthood by;
And I squeezed your fingers till you found again
My hand hidden in yours.

I squeeze your fingers:

Dick King was an upright man.
Sixty years he trod
The dull stations underfoot.
Fifteen he lies with God.

By the salt seaboard he grew up
But left its rock and rain
To bring a dying language east
And dwell in Basin Lane.

By the Southern Railway he increased:
His second soul was born
In the clangour of the iron sheds,
The hush of the late horn.

An invalid he took to wife.
She prayed her life away;
Her whisper filled the whitewashed yard
Until her dying day.

And season in, season out,
He made his wintry bed.
He took the path to the turnstile
Morning and night till he was dead.

He clasped his hands in a Union ward
To hear St James's bell.
I searched his eyes though I was young,
The last to wish him well.

# Cover Her Face

*She has died suddenly, aged twenty-nine years, in Dublin. Some of her family travel from the country to bring her body home. Having driven all morning through a storm*

## 1

They dither softly at her bedroom door
In soaking overcoats, and words forsake
Even their comforters. The bass of prayer
Haunts the chilly landing while they take
Their places in a murmur of heartbreak.

Shabby with sudden tears, they know their part,
Mother and brother, resigning all that ends
At these drab walls. For here, with panicked heart,
A virgin broke the seal; who understands
The sheet pulled white and Maura's locked blue hands?

Later her frown will melt, when by degrees
They flinch from grief. A girl they have never seen,
Sunk now in love and horror to her knees,
The black official giving discipline
To shapeless sorrow, these are more their kin,

By grace of breath, than that grave derelict
Whose blood and feature, like a sleepy host,
Agreed a while with theirs. Her body's tact
Swapped child for woman, woman for a ghost,
Until its buried sleep lay uppermost;

And Maura, come to terms at last with pain,
Rests in her ruptured mind, her temples tight,
Patiently weightless as her time burns down.
Soon her few glories will be shut from sight:
Her slightness, the fine metal of her hair spread out,

Her cracked, sweet laugh. Such gossamers as hold
Friends, family – all fortuitous conjunction –
Sever with bitter whispers; with untold
Peace shrivel to their anchors in extinction.
There, newly trembling, others grope for function.


## 2


Standing by the door, effaced in self,
I cannot deny her death, protest, nor grieve,
Dogged by a scrap of memory: some tossed shelf
Holds, a secret shared, that photograph,
Her arm tucked tiredly into mine; her laugh,

As though she also knew a single day
Would serve to bleed us to a diagram,
Sighs and confides. She waived validity
The night she drank the furnace of the Lamb,
Draining one image of its faint *I am*.

I watch her drift, in doubt whether dead or born
– Not with Ophelia's strewn virginity
But with a pale unmarriage – out of the worn
Bulk of day, under its sightless eye,
And close her dream in hunger. So we die.

Monday, without regret, darkens the pane
And sheds on the shaded living, the crystal soul,
A gloomy lustre of the pouring rain.
Nuns have prepared her for the holy soil
And round her bed the faded roses peel

That the fruit of justice may be sown in peace
To them that make peace, and bite its ashen bread.
Mother, brother, when our questions cease
Such peace may come, consenting to the good,
Chaste, biddable, out of all likelihood.

# Girl on a Swing

My touch has little force:
Her infant body falls.
Her lips lightly purse
With panic and delight
And fly up to kiss
The year's brimming glass;
To drink; to sag sweetly
When I drop from sight.


# A Country Walk

Sick of the piercing company of women,
I swung the gate shut with a furious sigh,
Rammed trembling hands in pockets and drew in
A breath of river air.
                        A rook's wet wing
Cuffed abruptly upward through the drizzle.

On either hand, dead trunks in drapes of creeper.
I walked their hushed stations, passion dying,
Each slow footfall a drop of peace returning.

I clapped my gloves. Three cattle turned aside
Their fragrant bodies from a corner gate,
Churning land to liquid in their passage.
Briefly through the beaded grass a path
Led to the holy stillness of a well,
And there in the smell of water, stone and leaf
I knelt, baring my hand, and scooped and drank.

And soon proceded with a lighter step
Down the river valley, wide and quiet.
An aqueduct on one horizon; rooted
In delicate ruin. On the opposite hill
A great asylum reared its potent calm.

A steeple; the long yielding of a railway turn
Through thorn and willow. Joining the two slopes,
Blocking an ancient way with barracks and brewery,
A town received the river. Lines of roofs
Fused in veils of mist and steely light.
A strand of idle smoke mounted until
An idler current combed it slowly West,
A hook of shadow dividing the still sky.

I passed a marshy field: that shallow ford
A place of bloodshed, as the tales agree.
There, the day that Christ hung dying, twin
Brothers armed in hate; the day darkened;
They crossed swords under a full eclipse
And mingled their bowels at the saga's end.
There the first Normans massacred my fathers
Then stroked their armoured horses' necks, disposed
In ceremony, sable on green sward.
Twice more the reeds grew red: when knot-necked Cromwell
Despatched a convent shrieking to their Lover;
And when a rebel host, through long retreat
Grown half hysterical – methodical, ludicrous –
Piked Cromwell's Puritan brood, their harmless neighbours,
In groups of three into the sharp water,
Then melted into the martyred countryside,
Root eaters, strange as badgers.

                        And my path
Passed a concrete cross low in the ditch.
– For one who answered latest the phantom Hag.
There he bled to death. And never saw
His town ablaze with joy; the grinning foe
Driven, in heavy lorries, from the field.
And he lay cold in the Hill Cemetery
When Freedom burned his comrades' itchy palms,
Too much for flesh and blood and, armed in hate,
Brother met brother in a modern light.

They turned the bloody corner, knelt and killed,
Who gather still at Easter round his grave,
Our watchful elders. Mixed among his bones
He takes their soil, and chatting they return

To take their town again, that have exchanged
A trenchcoat playground for a gombeen jungle.

Around the corner, in the Market Square,
I came upon the sombre monuments
That bear their names: MacDonagh and McBride,
Merchants; Connolly's Commercial Arms...
I walked their shopfronts, the declining light
Playing on lens and raincoat stonily,
And turned away.

                  On the far side of the Square
A lamp switched on above the urinal.
Across the silent handball alley, eyes
That never looked on lover measured mine
Over the Christian Brothers' frosted glass
And turned away.
                  Out of the neighbouring shades
A car plunged soundlessly and disappeared
Over the bridge. A dripping sycamore
Let fall from its combining arms a single
Word on my upturned face.
                  The parapet
Above the central arch received my hands.

*

Under a darkening and clearing heaven
The hastening river flowed in a slate sheen,
Its face a-swarm. A thousand currents broke,
Kissing, dismembering, in threads of foam
Or poured intact over the stony bed
Glass-green and chill. Their shallow, shifting waters
Slid on in troubled union, mixing together
Surfaces that gave and swallowed light.
And grimly the flood divided where it swept
An endless debris through the failing dusk
Under the trembling span beneath my feet.

*Venit Hesperus.*
In green and golden light.
                  Bringing sweet trade.

# Downstream

The West a fiery complex, the East a pearl,
We gave our frail skiff to the slow-moving stream,
Ruffling the waters. And steadied on a seam
Of calm and current.

                        Together, both as one,
We lifted our dripping blades in the dying light
And thrust ourselves forward, thrusting behind
Old willows with their shadows half undone
And groves of alder mowing like the blind.

A swan woke shapelessly in muffled stress
And thrust on ploughing wings, diminishing
Downstream.
                Ghost of whiteness.

We drifted in peace, and talked of poetry.
I opened the Cantos; and chose the silken kings,
Luminous with crisis, waging war
Among the primal clarities. Their names
Dying in the dusk.

                        I closed the book,
The gathering shades beginning to deceive,
And wiped the dewy cover on my sleeve.

                        *

We halted by a thorn, against the bank
Of a tributary stream. He clambered out;
I held on by a branch.

                        Night voices: soft
Lips of liquid, while the river swept
Its spectral surface by.

                        He coughed,
Standing against the sky. I took my turn,
Standing on the earth, staring aloft

At fields of light sprinkled in countless silence;
I named their shapes, above the Central Plain,
With primal thumb.

Low on the horizon
A shape of cloud answered with a soft flash
And a low word of thunder.

*

Toward Durrow Wood.

Thick slopes from shore to shore
Lowered a matted arch and moved out roots,
Full of slant pike, over the river floor.

The black cage closed about us:
furred night-brutes
Stopped and listened, twitching their tiny brushes.

And I remembered how, among those bushes,
A man one night fell sick and left his shell
Collapsed, half eaten, like a rotted thrush's

To frighten stumbling children. 'You could tell',
My co-shadow murmured, 'by the hands
He died in trouble.' And the cold of hell,

A limb-lightness, a terror in the glands,
Pierced again as when that story first
Stopped my blood. The soil of other lands

Drank lives that summer with a body thirst.
Nerveless by the European pit,
Ourselves through seven hundred years accurst,

We saw the barren world obscurely lit
By tall chimneys flickering in their pall,
The haunt of swinish man. Each day a spit

That, turning, sweated war. Each night a fall
Back to the evil dream where rodents ply,
Man-rumped, sow-headed, busy with whip and maul

Among nude herds of the damned. It seemed that I,
Coming to conscience on that edge of dread,
Still dreamed, impervious to calamity,

Imagining a formal drift of the dead
Stretched calm as effigies on velvet dust,
Scattered on starlit slopes with arms outspread

And eyes of silver... When that story thrust
Pungent horror and an actual mess
Into my very face, and taste I must.

*

Like mortal jaws, the alleys of the wood
Fell-to behind us. At their heart, a ghost
That glimmered briefly with my gift of blood,

Spreadeagled on a rack of leaves, almost
Remembering, facing the crowded sky,
Calmly encountering the starry host,

Meeting their silver eyes with silver eye,
An X of wavering flesh, a skull of light,
Fading in our wake without a sigh.

*

Soon the current shuddered in its flight
And swerved on pliant muscle. We were sped
Through sudden quiet into a pit of night

– The Mill Hole, its rocky fathoms fed
On moss and pure depth and the cold fin
Turning in its heart. The river bed

Called to our flesh, under the watery skin.
Our shell trembled in answer.
                                    A quiet hiss;

Something shifted in sleep; a milk-white breast.
A shift of wings betrayed with feathery kiss
A soul of white with darkness for a nest.

The creature bore the night so tranquilly
I lifted up my eyes. There without rest
The phantoms of the overhanging sky

Occupied their stations and descended.
Another moment, to the starlit eye,
The slow, downstreaming dead, it seemed, were blended

One with those silver hordes, and briefly shared
Their order, glittering. And then impended
A barrier of rock that turned and bared

A varied barrenness as toward its base
We glided – blotting heaven as it towered –
Searching the darkness for a landing place.


# Chrysalides

Our last free summer we mooned about at odd hours
Pedalling slowly through country towns, stopping to eat
Chocolate and fruit, tracing our vagaries on the map.

At night we watched in the barn, to the lurch of melodeon music,
The crunching boots of countrymen – huge and weightless
As their shadows – twirling and leaping over the yellow concrete.

Sleeping too little or too much, we awoke at noon
And were received with womanly mockery into the kitchen,
Like calves poking our faces in with enormous hunger.

Daily we strapped our saddlebags and went to experience
A tolerance we shall never know again, confusing
For the last time, for example, the licit and the familiar.

Our instincts blurred with change; a strange wakefulness
Sapped our energies and dulled our slow-beating hearts
To the extremes of feeling – insensitive alike

To the unique succession of our youthful midnights,
When by a window ablaze softly with the virgin moon
Dry scones and jugs of milk awaited us in the dark,

Or to lasting horror, a wedding flight of ants
Spawning to its death, a mute perspiration
Glistening like drops of copper, agonised, in our path.


# Mirror in February

The day dawns with scent of must and rain,
Of opened soil, dark trees, dry bedroom air.
Under the fading lamp, half dressed – my brain
Idling on some compulsive fantasy –
I towel my shaven jaw and stop, and stare,
Riveted by a dark exhausted eye,
A dry downturning mouth.

It seems again that it is time to learn,
In this untiring, crumbling place of growth
To which, for the time being, I return.
Now plainly in the mirror of my soul
I read that I have looked my last on youth
And little more; for they are not made whole
That reach the age of Christ.

Below my window the awakening trees,
Hacked clean for better bearing, stand defaced
Suffering their brute necessities,
And how should the flesh not quail that span for span
Is mutilated more? In slow distaste
I fold my towel with what grace I can,
Not young and not renewable, but man.

from

# *Wormwood*

## (1966)

## *Wormwood*

I have dreamt it again: standing suddenly still
In a thicket, among wet trees, stunned, minutely
Shuddering, hearing a wooden echo escape.

A mossy floor, almost colourless, disappears
In depths of rain among the tree shapes.
I am straining, tasting that echo a second longer.

If I can hold it…familiar if I can hold it.
A black tree with a double trunk – two trees
Grown into one – throws up its blurred branches.

The two trunks in their infinitesimal dance of growth
Have turned completely about one another, their join
A slowly twisted scar, that I recognise…

A quick arc flashes sidewise in the air,
A heavy blade in flight. A wooden stroke:
Iron sinks in the gasping core.

I will dream it again.

# First Light

A prone couple still sleeps.
Light ascends like a pale gas
Out of the sea: dawn-light
Reaching across the hill
To the dark garden. The grass
Emerges, soaking with grey dew.

Inside, in silence, an empty
Kitchen takes form, tidied and swept,
Blank with marriage – where shrill
Lover and beloved have kept
Another vigil far
Into the night, and raved and wept.

Upstairs a whimper or sigh
Comes from an open bedroom door
And lengthens to an ugly wail
– A child enduring a dream
That grows, at the first touch of day,
Unendurable.


# Remembering Old Wars

What clamped us together? When each night fell we lay down
In the smell of decay and slept, our bodies leaking,
Limp as the dead, breathing that smell all night.

Then light prodded us awake, and adversity
Flooded up from inside us as we laboured upright
Once more to face the hells of circumstance.

And so on, without hope of change or peace.
Each dawn, like lovers recollecting their purpose,
We would renew each other with a savage smile.

from

# Nightwalker and Other Poems

(1968)

## *Our Mother*

Tall windows full of sea light,
Two women and a child in tears
Silent among screens and flowers,
The ward a quiet zone of air.

The girl whimpers in bed, remote
Under the anaesthetic still.
She sleeps on her new knowledge, a bride
With bowels burning and disarrayed.

She dreams a red Gorgon-mask
Warped in the steel kidney dish,
The tender offals of her core
Worming around the raw stare.

Her mother watches, struck dumb.
Tears of recognition run
For the stranger, daughter, self, on whom
In fascination her eyes feed,

As mine on her – a revenant,
A rain-worn, delicate
Stone shape that has looked long
Into that other face direct.

In the next bed, dying of age,
The carrier of all our harm
Turns on us an emptiness
Of open mouth and damp eyes.

All three women, two in my care,
The third beyond all care, in tears.
Living, dying, I meet their stare
Everywhere, and cannot move.

## *Office for the Dead*

The grief-chewers enter, their shoes hard on the marble,
In white lace and black skirts, books held to their loins.
A silver pot tosses in its chains as they assemble
About the coffin, heavy under its cloth, and begin.

Back and forth, each side in nasal unison
Against the other, their voices grind across her body.
We watch, kneeling like children, and shrink as their Church
Latin chews our different losses into one

– All but certain images of her pain that will not,
In the coarse process, pass through the cloth and hidden boards
To their peace in the shroud; that delay, still real –

High thin shoulders – eyes boring out of the dusk –
Wistful misshapenness – a stripped, dazzling mouth –
Her frown as she takes the candle pushed into her hands
In the last crisis, propped up, dying with worry.

*Sanctus.* We listen with bowed heads to the thrash of chains
Measuring the silence. The pot gasps in its smoke.
An animal of metal, dragging itself and breathing.

# Ballydavid Pier

Noon. The luminous tide
Climbs through the heat, covering
Grey shingle. A film of scum
Searches first among litter,
Cloudy with (I remember)
Life; then crystal-clear shallows
Cool on the stones, silent
With shells and claws, white fish bones;
Farther out a bag of flesh,
Foetus of goat or sheep,
Wavers below the surface.

Allegory forms of itself:
The line of life creeps upward
Replacing one world with another,
The welter of its advance
Sinks down into clarity,
Slowly the more foul
Monsters of loss digest.

Small monster of true flesh
Brought forth somewhere
In bloody confusion and error
And flung into bitterness,
Blood washed white:
Does that structure satisfy?

The ghost tissue hangs unresisting
In allegorical waters,
Lost in self-search
– A swollen blind brow
Humbly crumpled over
Budding limbs, unshaken
By the spasms of birth or death.

The Angelus. Faint bell-notes
From some church in the distance
Tremble over the water.
It is nothing. The vacant harbour

Is filling; it will empty.
The misbirth touches the surface
And glistens like quicksilver.


# *Traveller*

Behind me my children vanish, left asleep
In their strange bed, in apple-tasted night.
I drive from worry to worry, to where my wife
Struggles for her breath in a private room.

An hour to midnight, and the traps of self
Are open for eighty solitary miles ahead,
In the swerving ditch, in the flash of tree-trunks and hedges.

The brain, woken to itself and restless,
Senses their black mouths muttering in the darkness:
Phrases, echoes of feeling, from other journeys
To bait and confuse the predatory will
And draw it aside, muttering in absent response,
Down stale paths in the dark to a stale lair,
In brainless trance, where it can treadle and chew
Old pangs blunter and smoother, old self-mutilations.

Far ahead on the road the lamps caught something.
A cat. A bird. Mesmerised. It moved,
Eating. It rose slowly, white furred, and flew
Up into the dark. An owl! My heart
Stood still. I had forgotten the very existence...

# Westland Row

We came to the outer light down a ramp in the dark
Through eddying cold gusts and grit, our ears
Stopped with noise. The hands of the station clock
Stopped, or another day vanished exactly.
The engine departing hammered slowly overhead.
Dust blowing under the bridge, we stooped slightly
With briefcases and books and entered the wind.

The savour of our days restored, dead
On nostril and tongue. Drowned in air,
We stepped on our own traces, not on stone,
Nodded and smiled distantly and followed
Our scattering paths, not stumbling, not touching.

Until, in a breath of benzine from a garage-mouth,
By the Academy of Music coming against us
She stopped an instant in her wrinkled coat
And ducked her childish cheek in the coat-collar
To light a cigarette: seeing nothing,
Thick-lipped, in her grim composure.

Daughterwife, look upon me.

# Folk Wisdom

Each year for a short season
The toads stare and wait
And clutch in their being
A shrieking without breath.
There is nothing but the harrow –
Everything speaks its approach;
Even blades of grass,
Flower stems, are harrows' teeth,
Hideous, because they are
Parallel and in earth.

The men are shackling their horses
In the yard. They talk softly
About earth and seed.

Soon the toads will shriek –
Each, as he hears his neighbour,
Gathers all his strength.

And so the curse was lifted,
According to the tale;
One kiss, and a prince stood there
Where a toad had been.

It is possible…such a strain,
Under the kiss of the harrow,
Could suffice. As when a man
Clutches his ears, deafened
By his world, to find a jewel
Made of pain in his hands.

# Before Sleep

It is time for bed. The cups and saucers are gathered
And stacked in the kitchen, the tray settled
With your tablets, a glass, a small jug of orange.
Are the windows shut, and all the doors locked?

I pass near the desk in my room and stand a minute
Looking down the notes I made this morning.
Yes: tomorrow it might do to begin.

The wall opposite is blank but alive
– Standing water over sunken currents.
The currents pursue their slow eddies through the house
Scarcely loosening as yet the objects of our love.

Soon the Falls will thunder, our love's detritus
Slide across the brim seriatim, glittering,
And vanish, swallowed into that insane
White roar. Chaos. All battered, scattered.

Yes: in the morning I will put on the cataract,
Give it veins, clutching hands, the short shriek of thought.

# Magnanimity

*for Austin Clarke's seventieth birthday*

       *'So I forgot*
*His enmity.'*
                 Green abundance
Last summer in Coole Park. A stone hearth
Surviving; a grassy path by the orchard wall.

You stared through chicken-wire at the initials
Cut in Lady Gregory's tree, scars grown thick.
Overhead a breath passed magniloquently through the leaves,

Branches swayed and sank. You turned away and said
Coole might be built again as a place for poets.
Through the forbidden tree magnanimity passed.


I am sure that there are no places for poets,
Only changing habitations for verse to outlast.
Your own house, isolated by a stream, exists

For your use while you live – like your body and your world.
Helpless commonness encroaches, chews the soil,
Squats ignobly. Within, consciousness intensifies:

Sharp small evils magnify into Evil,
Pity and mockery suggest some idea of Good,
Fright stands up stiffly under pain of death.


Houses shall pass away, and all give place
To signposts and chicken-wire.
                      A tree stands.
Pale cress persists on a shaded stream.

## The Poet Egan O'Rahilly, Homesick in Old Age

He climbed to his feet in the cold light, and began
The decrepit progress again, blown along the cliff road,
Bent with curses above the shrew his stomach.

The salt abyss poured through him, more raw
With every laboured, stony crash of the waves:
His teeth bared at their voices, that incessant dying.

Iris leaves bent on the ditch, unbent,
Shivering in the wind: leaf-like spirits
Chattered at his death-mark as he passed.

He pressed red eyelids: aliens crawled
Breaking princely houses in their jaws;
Their metal faces reared up, eating at light.

'Princes overseas, who slipped away
In your extremity, no matter where I travel
I find your great houses like stopped hearts.

Likewise your starving children – though I nourish
Their spirit, and my own, on the lists of praises
I make for you still in the cooling den of my craft.

Our enemies multiply. They have recruited the sea:
Last night, the West's rhythmless waves destroyed my sleep;
This morning, winkle and dogfish persisting in the stomach...'

# *Soft Toy*

I am soiled with the repetition of your loves and hatreds
    And other experiments. You do not hate me,
Crumpled in my corner. You do not love me,
    A small heaped corpse. My face of beaten fur
Responds as you please: if you do not smile
    It does not smile; to impatience or distaste
It answers blankness, beyond your goodwill
    – Blank conviction, beyond your understanding or mine.

I lie limp with use and re-use, listening.
    Loose ends of conversations, hesitations,
Half-beginnings that peter out in my presence,
    Are enough. I understand, with a flame of shame
Or a click of ease or joy, inert. Knowledge
    Into resignation: the process drives deeper,
Grows clearer, eradicating chance growths of desire.
    And colder: all possibilities of desire.

My button-brown hard eyes fix on your need
    To grow, as you crush me with tears and throw me aside.
Most they reflect, but something absorb – brightening
    In response, with energy, to the energy of your changes.
Clutched tightly through the night, held before you,
    Ragged and quietly crumpled, as you thrust, are thrust,
In dull terror into your opening brain,
    I face the dark with eyes that cannot close
– The cold, outermost points of your will, as you sleep.
    Between your tyrannous pressure and the black
Resistance of the void my blankness hardens
    To a blunt probe, a cold pitted grey face.

# Leaf-Eater

On a shrub in the heart of the garden,
On an outer leaf, a grub twists
Half its body, a tendril,
This way and that in blind
Space: no leaf or twig
Anywhere in reach; then gropes
Back on itself and begins
To eat its own leaf.


# Nightwalker

Mindful of the shambles of the day,
    But mindful, under the blood's drowsy humming,
Of will that gropes for structure; nonetheless
    Not unmindful of the madness without,
The madness within – the book of reason
    Slammed open, slammed shut:


## 1

I only know things seem and are not good.

A brain in the dark and bones out exercising
Shadowy flesh. Fitness for the soft belly,
Fresh air for lungs that take no pleasure any longer.
The smell of gardens under suburban lamplight;
Clipped privet; a wall blotted with shadows:
Monsters of ivy squat in lunar glare.

There above the roofs it hangs,
A mask of grey dismay, like a fat skull.
Or the pearl knob of a pendulum

At the outermost reach of its swing, about to detach
Its hold on the upper night, for the return.
That dark area the mark of Cain.

*

My shadow twists about my feet in the light
Of every passing street lamp. Window after window
Pale entities, motionless in their cells like grubs,
Stare in a blue trance.

A laboratory
Near Necropolis. Underground. Embalmers,
Their arms toil in unearthly light,
Their mouths opening and closing.

A shade enters.
Patrolling the hive of his brain.

*

I must lie down with them all soon and sleep,
And rise with them again when the new day
Has roused us. We'll come scratching in our waistcoats
Down to the kitchen for a cup of tea.
Then with our briefcases, by the neighbours' gardens,
To wait at the station, assembled for the day's toil,
Fluttering our papers, palping the cool wind.
Ready to serve our businesses and government
As together we develop our community
On clear principles, with no fixed ideas.
And (twitching our thin umbrellas) agreeable
That during a transitional period
Development should express itself in forms
Without principle, based on fixed ideas.

Robed in spattered iron she stands
At the harbour mouth, Productive Investment,
And beckons the nations through our gold half-door:
Lend me your wealth, your cunning and your drive,
Your arrogant refuse. Let my people serve them
Holy water in our new hotels,

While native businessmen and managers
Drift with them chatting over to the window
To show them our growing city, give them a feeling
Of what is possible; our labour pool,
The tax concessions to foreign capital,
How to get a nice estate though German.
Even collect some of our better young artists.

*

Our new constellations are rising into view
At the end of the terrace. You can pick them out,
With their pale influences.

The Wakeful Twins
                    *Bruder und Schwester...*
Two young Germans I had in this morning
Wanting to transfer investment income.
The sister a business figurehead, her brother
Otterfaced, with exasperated smiles
Assuming – pressing until he achieved – response.
Handclasp; I do not exist; I cannot take
My eyes from their pallor. A red glare
Plays on their faces, livid with little splashes
Of blazing fat. The oven door closes.

                    There: The Wedding Group...
The Groom, the Best Man, the Fox, and their three ladies.
A tragic tale.
                    Soon, the story tells,
Enmity sprang up between them, and the Fox
Took to the wilds. Then, to the Groom's sorrow,
His dear friend left him also, vowing hatred.
So they began destroying the Groom's substance
And he sent out to hunt the Fox, but trapped
His friend instead; mourning he slaughtered him.
Shortly in his turn the Groom was savaged
No one knows by whom. Though it's known the Fox
Is a friend of Death, and rues nothing.

                                And there, in the same quarter,
The Two Executioners – Groom and Weasel –
'77' burning onto each brow.


                                And there the Weasel again,
Dancing crookbacked under the Player King.
A tragicomical tale:
                                How the Fox discovered
A great complex gold horn left at his door;
Examined it with little curiosity,
Wanting no gold or music; observed the mouthpiece,
Impossible to play with fox's lips;
And gave it with dull humour to his old enemy,
The Weasel. Who bared his needle teeth,
Recognising the horn of the Player King.
He took it, hammered on it with a stick,
And pranced about in blithe pantomime,
His head cocked to enjoy the golden clouts.
While the Fox from time to time nodded his mask.




                              2


The human taste grows faint, leaving a taste
Of self and laurel leaves and rotted salt.
And gardens smelling of half-stripped rocks in the dark.

A cast-iron lamp standard on the sea wall
Sheds yellow light on a page of the day's paper
Turning in the gutter:
                              Our new young minister
Glares in his hunting suit, white haunch on haunch.

Other lamps are lighting along a terrace
Of high Victorian houses, toward the tower
Rising into the dark at the Forty Foot.
The tide drawing back from the promenade
Far as the lamplight can reach, into a dark
Alive with signals. Little bells clonk in the channel
Beyond the rocks; Howth twinkling across the Bay;

Ships' lights moving along invisible sea lanes;
The Bailey light sweeping the middle distance,
Flickering on something.

*

                    Watcher in the tower,
Be with me now. Turn your milky spectacles
On the sea, unblinking.

                    A dripping cylinder
Pokes up into sight, picked out by the moon.
Two blazing eyes. Two tough shoulders of muscle
Lit from within by joints and bones of light.
Another head: animal, with nostrils
Straining open, red as embers. Goggle eyes.
A phantom whinny. Forehooves scrape at the night.
A spectral stink of horse and rider's sweat.
The rider grunts and urges.

                    Father of Authors!
It is himself! In silk hat, accoutred
In stern jodhpurs. The Sonhusband
Coming in his power, climbing the dark
To his mansion in the sky, to take his place
In the influential circle, mounting to glory
On his big white harse!

                    A new sign: Foxhunter.
Subjects will find the going hard but rewarding.
You may give offence, but this should pass.
Marry the Boss's daughter.

*

The soiled paper settles back in the gutter.
THE NEW IRELAND...
                    Awkward in the saddle

But able and willing for the foul ditch,
And sitting as well as any at the kill,
Whatever iron Faust opens the gate.

It is begun: curs mill and yelp at your heel,
Backsnapping and grinning. They eye your back.
Beware the smile of the dog.

                    But you know the breed,
And all it takes to turn them
To a pack of lickspittles running as one.


## 3

The foot of the tower. An angle where the darkness
Is complete. A backdrop of constellations,
Crudely done and mainly unfamiliar.
They are arranged to suggest a chart of the brain.

In the part of the little harbour that can be seen
The moon is reflected in low water. Beyond,
A line of lamps on the terrace.

                    From the vest's darkness,
Smell of my body; faint brutality;
Chalk dust and flowers.

                    Music far off.
The loins of Brother Burke
Flattened in his soutane against my desk:

… And Dublin Castle used the National Schools
To try to conquer the Irish national spirit
At the same time exterminating our 'jargon'
– The Irish language, in which Saint Patrick, Saint Bridget
And Saint Colmcille taught and prayed!

Edmund Ignatius Rice founded our Order
To provide schools that were national in more than name.
Pupils from our schools have played their part
In the fight for freedom. And you will be called
 In your various ways.

                    To show your love
By working for your language and your country.
Today there are past pupils everywhere
In the Government service. Ministers of State
Have sat where some of you are sitting now.

The Blessed Virgin smiles from her pedestal
Like young Victoria. Celibates, adolescents,
We make our vows to God and Ireland; thankful
That by our studies here they may not lack
Civil Servants in a state of grace.


                         *


A seamew passes over, whingeing: *Eire,*
*Eire. Is there none to hear? Is all lost?*
*Alas, I think I will dash myself at the stones.*

*I will become a wind on the sea again.*
*Or a wave of the sea,*
                         *or a sea sound.*

*At the first light of the sun I stirred on my rock.*
*I have seen the sun go down at the end of the world.*
*Now I fly across the face of the moon.*


A dying language echoes
                         across a century's silence.


                         4


Moon of my dismay, Virgin most pure,
Reflected enormous in her shaggy pool,
Quiet as oil. My brain swims in her light
And gathers into a book beneath her stare.
She reads and her mask darkens.
But she soon brightens a little:

It was a terrible time.
Nothing but horrors of one kind or another.
My tears flowed again and again.
But we came to take the waters, and when I drank
I felt my patience and trust coming back.

From time to time it seems that everything
Is breaking down. But we must never despair.
There are times it is all part of a meaningful drama
Beginning in the grey mists of antiquity
And reaching through the years to unknown goals
In the consciousness of man, which makes it less gloomy.

A wind sighs. The pool shivers. The tide
At the turn. An odour of the sea bed.
She rules on high, queenlike, pale with control.


Hatcher of peoples!
Incline out of your darkness into mine.
I stand at the ocean's edge,
My head fallen back heavy with your control,
And oppressed.



5

          A pulse hisses in my ear.
I am an arrow piercing the void, unevenly
As I correct and correct. But swift as thought.

I arrive enveloped in quiet.
                              A true desert,
Sterile and odourless. Naked to every peril.

A bluish light beats down,
To kill every bodily thing.
But the shadows are alive.

They scuttle and flicker across the surface,
Searching for any sick spirits,
To suck at the dry juices.

If I stoop down and touch the dust
It has a human taste:
                    massed human wills.

I believe
          I have heard of this place. I think
This is the Sea of Disappointment.

                    *


It is time I turned for home.

Her dear shadow on the blind.
The breadknife. She was slicing and buttering
A loaf of bread. My heart stopped. I starved for speech.

I believe now that love is half persistence,
A medium in which from change to change
Understanding may be gathered.

Hesitant, cogitating, exit.

# Ritual of Departure

## 1

Open the soft string that clasps in series
A dozen silver spoons, and spread them out,
Matched perfectly, one maker and to the year,
Brilliant in use from the first inheritor.

A stag crest stares from the soft solid silver
With fat cud lips and jaws that could crack bones.
The stag heart stumbles, rearing at bay,
Rattling a trophied head, slavering silver.

*

A portico, beggars moving on the steps.
A horserider locked in soundless greeting,
Bowed among dogs and dung. A panelled vista
Closing on pleasant smoke-blue far-off hills.

The same city distinct in the same air,
More open in an earlier evening light,
In sweet-breathing death-ease after forced Union.
Domes, pillared, in the afterglow.

## 2

The ground opens. Pale wet potatoes
Fall into light. The black soil falls from their flesh,
From the hands that tear them up and spread them out,
Perishable roots to eat.

Fields dying away
Among white rock and red bog – saturated
High places traversed by spring sleet,
Thrust up through the thin wind into pounding silence.

Farther South: landscape with ancestral figures.
Names settling and intermixing on the earth.
The seed in slow retreat into bestial silence.
Faces sharpen and grow blank, with eyes for nothing.

*

And their children's children vanished in the city lanes.

I saw the light enter from the laneway
Through the scullery, and creep to the foot of the stairs
Over grey floorboards, and sink in plush
In the staleness of an inner room.

I scoop at the earth and sense famine,
A sourness in the clay. The roots tear softly.

3

A man at the moment of departure, turning
To leave, treasures some stick of furniture
With slowly blazing eyes, or the very door
Broodingly with his hand as it falls shut.

# Phoenix Park

*The Phaenix builds the Phaenix' nest.*
*Love's architecture is his own.*

## 1

One stays or leaves. The one who returns is not
The one, etcetera. And we are leaving.
You are quiet and watchful, this last visit.
We pass the shapes of cattle blurred by moisture;
A few deer lift up their wet horns from the grass;

A smoke-soft odour of graves... our native damp.
A twig with two damp leaves drops on the bonnet
From the upper world, trembling; shows us its clean
Fracture and vanishes, snatched off by the wind:
Droplets of moisture shudder on the windscreen.

– You start at the suddenness, as though it were
Your own delicate distinct flesh that had snapped.
What was in your thoughts... saying, after a while,
I write you nothing, no love songs, any more?
*Fragility echoing fragilities...*

The Chapelizod Gate. Dense trees on our right,
Sycamores and chestnuts around the entrance
To St Mary's Hospital. Under their shade
I entered long ago, took the twisting paths
To find you by the way of hesitation.

You lay still, brilliant with illness, behind glass;
I stooped and tasted your life until you woke,
And your body's fever leaped out at my mind.
There's a fever now that eats everything
– Everything but the one positive dream.

That dream: it is something I might offer you.
Sorry it is not anything for singing;
Your body would know that it is positive
– Everything you know you know bodily.
And the preparation also. Take them both.


### *The preparation*

Near a rounded wooded hillock, where a stream
Drains under the road, inside Islandbridge Gate,
A child stooped to the grass, picking and peeling
And devouring mushrooms straight out of the ground:
Death-pallor in their dry flesh, the taste of death.

Later, in freezing darkness, I came alone
To the railings round the Pond; whispered *Take me,*
*I am nothing.* But the words hovered, their sense
Revealing opposite within opposite.
Understanding moved, a silent bright discus.

As, when I walked this glimmering road, it did
Once, between night-trees. The stars seemed in my grasp,
Changing places among the naked branches
– Thoughts drawing into order under night's skull.
But something moved on the path: faint, sweet breathing –

A woman stood, thin and tired, in a light dress,
And interrupted kindly, in vague hunger.
Her hand rested for a moment on my sleeve.
I studied her and saw shame does not matter,
Nor kindness when there's no answering hunger

And passed by; her eyes burned… So equipped to learn
I found you, in feverish sleep, where you lay.
Midsummer, and I had tasted your knowledge,
My flesh blazing in yours; Autumn, I had learned
Giving without tearing is not possible.

\*

The Furry Glen: grass sloping down to the lake,
Where she stooped in her Communion finery,
Our first-born, Sara in innocence, and plucked
Something out of the ground for us to admire.
The child smiled in her white veil, self-regarding.


## 2

We leave the Park through the Knockmaroon Gate and turn,
Remembering, downhill to the Liffey road
With the ache of dampness growing in our lungs.
Along river curves sunk under heavy scenes,
By the Strawberry Beds, under gravel slopes,

To sit drinking in a back bar in Lucan
At a glass table, under a staring light,
Talking of departure. You are uneasy;
I make signs on the surface with my wet glass
In human regret, but human certainty:

Whatever the ultimate grotesqueries
They'll have to root in more than this sour present.
The ordeal-cup, set at each turn, so far
We have welcomed, sour or sweet. What matter where
It waits for us next, if we will take and drink?


*The dream*

Look into the cup: the tissues of order
Form under your stare. The living surfaces
Mirror each other, gather everything
Into their crystalline world. Figure echoes
Figure faintly in the saturated depths;

Revealed by faint flashes of each other
They light the whole confines: a fitful garden...
A child plucks death and tastes it; a shade watches
Over him, the child fades and the shade, made flesh,
Stumbles on understanding, begins to fade,

Bequeathing a child in turn; women-shapes pass
Unseeing, full of knowledge, through each other
... All gathered. And the crystal so increases,
Eliciting in its substance from the dark
The slowly forming laws its increases by.

Laws of order I find I have discovered
Mainly at your hands. Of failure and increase.
The stagger and recovery of spirit:
That life is hunger, hunger is for order,
And hunger satisfied brings on new hunger

Till there's nothing to come; – let the crystal crack
On some insoluble matter, then its heart
Shudders and accepts the flaw, adjusts on it
Taking new strength – given the positive dream;
Given, with your permission, undying love.

That, while the dream lasts, there's a total hunger
That gropes out disappearing just past touch,
A blind human face burrowing in the void,
Eating new tissue down into existence
Until every phantasm – all that can come –

Has roamed in flesh and vanished, or passed inward
Among the echoing figures to its place,
And this live world is emptied of its hunger
While the crystal world, undying, crowds with light,
Filling the cup... That there is one last phantasm

Who'll come painfully in old lewd nakedness
– Loose needles of bone coming out through his fat –
Groping with an opposite, equal hunger,
Thrusting a blind skull from its tatters of skin
As from a cowl, to smile in understanding

And total longing; aching to plant one kiss
In the live crystal as it aches with fullness,
And accommodate his body with that kiss;
But that forever he will pause, the final
Kiss ungiveable. Giving without tearing

Is not possible; to give totality
Is to be torn totally, a nothingness
Reaching out in stasis a pure nothingness.
– Therefore everlasting life, the unmoving
Stare of full desire. Given undying love.

*

I give them back not as your body knows them
– That flesh is finite, so in love we persist;
That love is to clasp simply, question fiercely;
That getting life we eat pain in each other.
But mental, in my fever – mere idea.

### 3

Our glasses drained, we finish and rise to go,
And stand again in the saturated air
Near the centre of the village, breathing in
Faint smells of chocolate and beer, fallen leaves
In the gutter, bland autumnal essences.

You wait a minute on the path, absently
– Against massed brown trees – tying a flimsy scarf
At your neck. Fair Elinor. O Christ thee save.
And I taste a structure, ramshackle, ghostly,
Vanishing on my tongue, given and taken,

Distinct. A ghost of that ghost persists, structure
Without substance, all about us, in the air,
Among the trees, before us at the crossroads,
On the stone bridge, insinuating itself
Into being. Undying…And I shiver

Seeing your thoughtless delicate completeness.
Love, it is certain, continues till we fail,
Whenever (with your forgiveness) that may be
– At any time, now, totally, ordeal
Succeeding ordeal till we find some death,

Hoarding bitterness, or refusing the cup;
Then the vivifying eye clouds, and the thin
Mathematic tissues loosen, and the cup
Thickens, and order dulls and dies in love's death
And melts away in a hungerless no dream.

*Fragility echoing fragilities*
*From whom I have had every distinctness*
*Accommodate me still, where – folded in peace*
*And undergoing with ghostly gaiety*
*Inner immolation, shallowly breathing –*

*You approach the centre by its own sweet light.*
*I consign my designing will stonily*
*To your flames. Wrapped in that rosy fleece, two lives*
*Burn down around one love, one flickering-eyed*
*Stone self becomes more patient than its own stone.*


## 4

The road divides and we can take either way,
Etcetera. The Phoenix Park; Inchicore,
Passing Phoenix Street – the ways are one, sweet choise,
*Our selves become our own best sacrifice.*
Continue, so. We'll perish in each other.

\*

The tyres are singing, cornering back and forth
In our green world again; into groves of trees,
By lake and open park, past the hospital.
The west ignites behind us; round one more turn
Pale light in the east hangs over the city:

An eighteenth-century prospect to the sea –
River haze; gulls; spires glitter in the distance
Above faint multitudes. Barely audible
A murmur of soft, wicked laughter rises.
Dublin, the umpteenth city of confusion.

A theatre for the quick articulate,
The agonized genteel, their artful watchers.
Malice as entertainment. Asinine feast
Of sowthistles and brambles! And there dead men,
Half hindered by dead men, tear down dead beauty.

Return by the mental ways we have ourselves
Established, past visages of memory
Set at every turn: where we smiled and passed
Without a second thought, or stood in the rain
And whispered bitterly; where we roamed at night

Drunk in joyful love, looking for enemies
('They in our bodies – white handkerchief, white page,
Crimsoned with panic); where naked by firelight
We stood and rested from each other and took
Our burden from the future, eyes crystalline,

My past alive in you, a gift of tissue
Torn free from my life in an odour of books.
That room… The shapes of tiredness had assembled
Long ago in its four dark corners, before
You came, waiting, while you were everywhere.

One midnight at the starlit sill I let them
Draw near. Loneliness drew into order:
A thought of fires in the hearts of darknesses,
A darkness at the heart of every fire,
Darkness, fire, darkness, threaded on each other –

The orders of stars fixed in abstract darkness,
Darknesses of worlds sheltering in their light;
World darkness harbouring orders of cities,
Whose light at midnight harbours human darkness;
The human dark pierced by solitary fires…

Such fires as one I have seen gutter and fail
And, as it sank, reveal the fault in its heart
Opening on abstract darkness, where hunger
Came with gaping kiss over terrible wastes
– Till the flames sprang up and blindness was restored.

Attracted from the night by my wakefulness
Certain half-dissolved – half-formed – beings loomed close:
A child with eaten features eating something –
Another, with unfinished features, in white –
They hold hands. A shadow bends to protect them.

The shadow tries to speak, but its tongue stumbles.
A snake out of the void moves in my mouth, sucks
At triple darkness. A few ancient faces
Detach and begin to circle. Deeper still,
Delicate distinct tissue begins to form.

from

# New Poems

(1973)

## *Hen Woman*

The noon heat in the yard
smelled of stillness and coming thunder.
A hen scratched and picked at the shore.
It stopped, its body crouched and puffed out.
The brooding silence seemed to say 'Hush…'

The cottage door opened,
a black hole
in a whitewashed wall so bright
the eyes narrowed.
Inside, a clock murmured 'Gong…'

(I had felt all this before.)

She hurried out in her slippers
muttering, her face dark with anger,
and gathered the hen up jerking
languidly. Her hand fumbled.
Too late. Too late.

It fixed me with its pebble eyes
(seeing what mad blur).
A white egg showed in the sphincter;
mouth and beak opened together;
and time stood still.

Nothing moved: bird or woman,
fumbled or fumbling – locked there
(as I must have been) gaping.

*

There was a tiny movement at my feet,
tiny and mechanical; I looked down.
A beetle like a bronze leaf
was inching across the cement,
clasping with small tarsi
a ball of dung bigger than its body.

The serrated brow pressed the ground humbly,
lifted in a short stare, bowed again;
the dung-ball advanced minutely,
losing a few fragments,
specks of staleness and freshness.

*

A mutter of thunder far off
– time not quite stopped.
I saw the egg had moved a fraction:
a tender blank brain
under torsion, a clean new world.

As I watched, the mystery completed.
The black zero of the orifice
closed to a point
and the white zero of the egg hung free,
flecked with greenish brown oils.

It fell and turned over slowly.
Dreamlike, fussed by her splayed fingers,
it floated outward, moon-white,
leaving no trace in the air,
and began its drop to the shore.

*

I feed upon it still, as you see;
there is no end to that which, not understood,
may yet be hoarded in the imagination,
in the yolk of one's being, so to speak,
there to undergo its (quite animal) growth,

dividing blindly, twitching, packed with will,
searching in its own tissue
for the structure in which it may wake.
Something that had – clenched in its cave –
not been now was: an egg of being.

Through what seemed a whole year it fell
– as it still falls, for me, solid and light,
the red gold beating in its silvery womb,
alive as the yolk and white of my eye.
As it will continue to fall, probably, until I die,
through the vast indifferent spaces
with which I am empty.

*

It smashed against the grating
and slipped down quickly out of sight.
It was over in a comical flash.
The soft mucous shell clung a little longer,
then drained down.

She stood staring, in blank anger.
Then her eyes came to life, and she laughed
and let the bird flap away.

'It's all the one.
There's plenty more where that came from!'

# A Hand of Solo

Lips and tongue
wrestle the delicious
    life out of you.

A last drop.
Wonderful.
    A moment's rest.

In the firelight glow
the flickering
    shadows softly

come and go up on the shelf:
red heart and black spade
    hid in the kitchen dark.

Woman throat song
help my head
    back to you sweet.

                    *

Hushed, buried green baize.
Slide and stop. Black spades. Tray. Still.
Red deuce. Two hearts. Blood-clean. Still.

Black flash. Jack Rat grins.
She drops down. Silent. Face disk blank. Queen.


The Boss spat in the kitchen fire.
His head shook.

Angus's fat hand brushed in all the pennies.
His waistcoat pressed the table.

Uncle Matty slithered the cards together
and knocked them. Their edges melted. Soft gold.

Angus picked up a bright penny and put it
in my hand: satiny, dream-new disk of light...

'Go on out in the shop and get yourself something.'
'Now Angus...'
                              'Now, now, Jack. He's my luck.'
'Tell your grandmother we're waiting for her.'


She was settling the lamp.
Two yellow tongues rose and brightened.
The shop brightened.

Her eyes glittered.
A tin ghost beamed, Mick McQuaid
nailed across the fireplace.

'Shut the kitchen door, child of grace.
Come here to me.
Come here to your old grandmother.'

Strings of jet beads wreathed her neck
and hissed on the black taffeta
and crept on my hair.

My eyes were squeezed shut against the key
in the pocket of her apron. Her stale abyss...
'...You'd think I had three heads!'

Old knuckles pressed on the counter,
then were snatched away. She sat down at the till
on her high stool, chewing nothing.


The box of Indian apples
was over in the corner
by the can of oil.

I picked out one of the fruit,
a rose-red hard wax
turning toward gold, light like wood,

and went at it with little bites,
peeling off bits of skin
and tasting the first traces of the blood.

When it was half peeled,
with the glassy pulp exposed like cells,
I sank my teeth in it

loosening the packed mass of dryish beads
from their indigo darkness.
I drove my tongue among them

and took a mouthful, and slowly
bolted them. My throat filled
with a rank, Arab bloodstain.


## *Ancestor*

I was going up to say something,
and stopped. Her profile against the curtains
was old, and dark like a hunting bird's.

It was the way she perched on the high stool,
staring into herself, with one fist
gripping the side of the barrier around her desk
– or her head held by something, from inside.
And not caring for anything around her
or anyone there by the shelves.
I caught a faint smell, musky and queer.

I may have made some sound – she stopped rocking
and pressed her fist in her lap; then she stood up
and shut down the lid of the desk, and turned the key.
She shoved a small bottle under her aprons
and came toward me, darkening the passageway.

Ancestor... among sweet- and fruit-boxes.
Her black heart...
                    Was that a sigh?
– brushing by me in the shadows,
with her heaped aprons, through the red hangings
to the scullery, and down to the back room.


# *Tear*


I was sent in to see her.
A fringe of jet drops
chattered at my ear
as I went in through the hangings.

I was swallowed in chambery dusk.
My heart shrank
at the smell of disused
organs and sour kidney.

The black aprons I used to          ·
bury my face in
were folded at the foot of the bed
in the last watery light from the window

(Go in and say goodbye to her)
and I was carried off
to unfathomable depths.
I turned to look at her.

She stared at the ceiling
and puffed her cheek, distracted,
propped high in the bed
resting for the next attack.

The covers were gathered close
up to her mouth,
that the lines of ill-temper still
marked. Her grey hair

was loosened out like a young woman's
all over the pillow,
mixed with the shadows
criss-crossing her forehead

and at her mouth and eyes,
like a web of strands tying down her head
and tangling down toward the shadow
eating away the floor at my feet.

I couldn't stir at first, nor wished to,
for fear she might turn and tempt me
(my own father's mother)
with open mouth

– with some fierce wheedling whisper –
to hide myself one last time
against her, and bury my
self in her drying mud.

Was I to kiss her? As soon
kiss the damp that crept
in the flowered walls
of this pit.

Yet I had to kiss.
I knelt by the bulk of the death bed
and sank my face in the chill
and smell of her black aprons.

Snuff and musk, the folds against my eyelids,
carried me into a derelict place
smelling of ash: unseen walls and roofs
rustled like breathing.

I found myself disturbing
dead ashes for any trace
of warmth, when far off
in the vaults a single drop

splashed. And I found
what I was looking for
– not heat nor fire,
not any comfort,

but her voice, soft, talking to someone
about my father: 'God help him, he cried
big tears over there by the machine
for the poor little thing.' Bright

drops on the wooden lid
for my infant sister.
My own wail of child-animal grief
was soon done, with any early guess

at sad dullness and tedious pain
and lives bitter with hard bondage.
How I tasted it now –
her heart beating in my mouth!

She drew an uncertain breath
and pushed at the clothes
and shuddered tiredly.
I broke free

and left the room
promising myself
when she was really dead
I would really kiss.

My grandfather half looked up
from the fireplace as I came out,
and shrugged and turned back
with a deaf stare to the heat.

I fidgeted beside him for a minute
and went out to the shop.
It was still bright there
and I felt better able to breathe.

Old age can digest
anything: the commotion
at Heaven's gate – the struggle
in store for you all your life.

How long and hard it is
before you get to Heaven,
unless like little Agnes
you vanish with early tears.

# The High Road

Don't be too long now, the next time.
She hugged me tight in behind the counter.
Here! she whispered.
                     A silvery
little mandoline, out of the sweet-box.

They were standing waiting in the sun outside
at the shop door, with the go car,
their long shadows along the path.

A horse trotted past us down Bow Lane:
Padno Carty sat in the trap
sideways, fat, drifting along
with a varnish twinkle of spokes
and redgold balls of manure scattering
behind on the road.

Mrs Fullerton was sitting on a stool
in her doorway, beak-nosed, one eye dead.
DAAARK! squawked the sour parrot in her room.
Sticking to his cage with slow nails, upside down;
creeping stiffly crossways, with his tongue
mumbling on a bar, a black moveable nut.

Silvery tiny strings
trembled in my brain.

Over the parapet of the bridge
at the end of Granny and Granda's
the brown water bubbled and poured
over the stones and tin cans in the Camac,
down by the back of Aunty Josie's.

After the bridge, a stony darkness
trickled down Cromwell's Quarters step by step,
along the foot of the wall from James's Street.
Through a barred window on one of the steps
a mob of shadows huddled in the Malt Stores
among the brick pillars and the dunes of grain.
Watching the pitch drain out of their wounds.

I held hands up the High Road
inside on the path, beside the feathery grass,
and looked down through the paling, pulled downward
by a queer feeling. Down there...windows
below the road. Small front gardens
getting lower and lower.
                              Over on the other side
a path slants up across the clay slope
and disappears into the Robbers' Den.
I crept up once to the big hole, full of fright,
and knelt on the clay to look inside.
It was only a hollow someone made,
with a dusty piece of man's dung, and bluebottles.

Not even in my mind
has one silvery string
picked a single sound.
And it will never.

*from* NEW POEMS (1973)

Over the far-off back yards
the breeze gave a sigh: a sin happening.
I let go and stopped, and looked down
and let it fall into empty air
and watched it turning over with little flashes
silveryshivering with loss.

## from *From the Land of the Dead*

### Touching the River

That nude kneeling so sad-seeming
on her shelf of moss
how timelessly – all sepia –
her arm reaches down
to let her fingers, affectedly trailing,
stick in the stopped brown water.

Rivery movement, clay-fresh;
light murmuring over the surface
as we kneel on the brink and drive our stare
down, now, into the current.
Our unstopped flesh and senses
– how they vanish!

### At the Crossroads

A dog's
body zipped
open and
stiff in
the grass.

They used to leave hanged men here.

A night when the moon is full
and swims with evil through the trees,
if you walk from the silent stone bridge
to the first crossroads and stand there,
do you feel that sad disturbance under the branches?
Three times I have been halted there
and had to whisper 'O Christ protect'
and not known whether my care was for myself
or some other hungry spirit.
Once by a great whiplash without sound.
Once by an unfelt shock at my ribs
as a phantom dagger stuck shuddering in nothing.
Once by a torch flare crackling
suddenly unseen in my face.
Three times, always at that same corner.
Never altogether the same. But the same.

Once when I had worked like a dull ox
in patience to the point of foolishness
I found myself rooted here, my thoughts
scattered by the lash Clarity:
the end of labour is in sacrifice,
the beast of burden in his shuddering prime
– or in leaner times any willing dogsbody.

A white face
stared from the
void, tilted over,
her mouth ready.

And all mouths everywhere so
in their need, turning on each furious
other. Flux of forms
in a great stomach: living meat torn off,
enduring in one mess of terror
every pang it sent through every thing
it ever, in shudders of pleasure, tore.

A white ghost flickered into being
and disappeared near the tree tops.
An owl in silent scrutiny
with blackness in her heart. She
who succeeds from afar…

              The choice –
the drop with deadened wing-beats; some creature
torn and swallowed; her brain, afterward,
staring among the rafters in the dark
until hunger returns.


## Sacrifice

Crowded steps, a sea of white faces
streaked with toil. The scrutiny is over,
in sunlight, terrible black and white.
There is the mark… In those streaks.
Their hands are on her.
Her friends gather.

The multitudes sigh and bless
and persuade her forward to her tears
in doomed excitement down the cup of light
onto her back on the washed bricks
with breasts held apart
and midriff fluttering in the sun.

The souls gather unseen, hovering
above the table, not interfering,
as it is done in a shivering flash.
The vivid pale solid of the breast
dissolves in a crimson flood.
The heart flops in its sty.

              *

Never mind the hurt. I've never felt
so terribly alive, so gripped by love
– gloved fingers slippery next the heart!

The blinding pain, when love goes direct!
But the pangs quickly pass their maximum,
and then such a fount of tenderness!

I love how you keep muttering 'You know now...'
– and your concern.
                    But you must finish it:

we are each other's knowledge;
it is peace that counts,
and knowledge brings peace,

even thrust crackling into the skull
and bursting with tongues of fire.
Peace. Love dying down, as love ascends.

I love your tender triumph, straightening up,
lifting your reddened sleeves.
The stain spreads downward

through your great flushed pinions.
You are a real angel.
My heart is in your hands; mind it well.


**All is emptiness
and I must spin**

A vacancy in which, apparently,
I hang
            with severed senses.

*

I have been in places... The floors crept,
an electric terror waited everywhere.
We were made to separate and strip.
My urine flowed in mild excitement.
Our hands touched in farewell.

How bring oneself to judge, or think,
so hurled onward! inward!

After a while there was a slight
but perceptible movement of the air.
It was not Death, but night.
Mountain coolness; a freshness of dew
on the face – tears of self forming.

*

I was lying in a vaulted place.
The cold air crept over long-abandoned floors,
carrying a taint of remote iron and dead ash.
Echo of voices. A distant door closed.

The sterile:
it is a whole matter in itself.

### Death Bed

Motionless – his sons –
we watched his brows draw together with strain.
The wind tore at the leather walls of our tent;
two grease lamps fluttered
at the head and foot of the bed.
Our shadows sprang here and there.

At that moment our sign might
have coursed across the heavens,
and we had spared no one to watch.

*

Our people are most vulnerable to loss
when we gather like this to one side,
around some death,

and try to weave it into our lives
– who can weave nothing but our ragged
routes across the desert.

And it is those among us
who most make the heavens their business
who go most deeply into this death-weaving.

As if the star might
spring from the dying mouth
or shoot from the agony of the eyes.

'We must not miss it,
however it comes.'
If it comes.

*

He stretched out his feet
and seemed to sink deeper in the bed,
and was still.

      Sons no longer,
we pulled down his eyelids
and pushed the chin up gently to close his mouth,
and stood under the flapping roof.
Our shelter sheltered under the night.

*

Hides, furs and skins,
are our shelter and our garments.

We can weave nothing.


### The Dispossessed

The lake is deserted now
but the water is still clean and transparent,
the headlands covered with laurels,
the little estuaries full of shells,
with enchanting parterres where the waves
ebb and flow over masses of turf and flowers.

It was like a miracle, a long pastoral, long ago.
The intoxication of a life gliding away
in the face of heaven: Spring,
a plain of flowers; Autumn, with grape-clusters
and chestnuts formed in its depths;
our warm nights passing under starlight.

We had established peace,
having learned to practise virtue
without expectation of recompense
– that we must be virtuous without hope.
(The Law is just; observe it,
maintain it, and it will bring contentment.)

Then, by the waterside, among the tortoises
with their mild and lively eyes, with crested larks
fluttering around Him, so light
they rested on a blade of grass
without bending it, He came among us
and lifted His unmangled hand:

These beauties, these earth-flowers growing and blowing,
what are they?
                    The spectacle of your humiliation!
If a man choose to enter the kingdom of peace
he shall not cease from struggle until he fail,
and having failed he will be astonished,
and having been astonished will rule,
and having ruled will rest.

Our dream curdled. We awoke
and began to thirst for the restoration of our house.
One morning, in a slow paroxysm of rage,
we found His corpse stretched on the threshold.

# *The Route of* The Táin

Gene sat on a rock, dangling our map.
The others were gone over the next crest,
further astray. We ourselves, irritated,
were beginning to turn down toward the river
back to the car, the way we should have come.

We should have trusted our book.
After they tried a crossing, and this river too
'rose against them' and bore off
a hundred of their charioteers toward the sea
*They had to move along the river Colptha*
*up to its source.*
                    There:
where the main branch sharpens away gloomily
to a gash in the hill opposite.

*then to Bélat Ailiúin*
                    by that pathway
climbing back and forth out of the valley
over to Ravensdale.

Scattering in irritation. Who had set out
so cheerfully to celebrate our book;
cheerfully as we made and remade it
through a waste of hours, content to 'enrich the present
honouring the past', each to his own just function.
Wandering off, ill-sorted,
like any beasts of the field,
one snout honking disconsolate,
another burrowing in its pleasures.

When not far above us a red fox
ran at full stretch out of the bracken
and panted across the hillside toward the next ridge.
Where he vanished – a faint savage sharpness
out of the earth – an inlet of the sea
shone in the distance at the mouth of the valley
beyond Omeath: grey waters crawled with light.

*from* NEW POEMS (1973)

For a heartbeat, in alien certainty,
we exchanged looks. We should have known it by now
– the process, the whole tedious enabling ritual.
Flux brought to fullness; saturated;
the clouding over; dissatisfaction
spreading slowly like an ache;
something reduced shivering suddenly
into meaning along new boundaries;

through a forest,
by a salt-dark shore,
by a standing stone on a dark plain,
by a ford running blood,
and along this gloomy pass, with someone ahead
calling and waving on the crest
against a heaven of dismantling cloud,
transfixed by the same figure (stopped, pointing)
on the rampart at Cruachan, where it began.

The morning sunlight pouring on us all
as we scattered over the mounds
disputing over useless old books,
assembled in cheerful speculation
around a prone block, *Miosgán Medba*
– Queen Medb's *turd*...? And rattled our maps,
joking together in growing illness
or age or fat. Before us
the route of the *Táin*, over men's dust,
toward these hills that seemed to grow
darker as we drove nearer.

# Ely Place

'Such a depth of charm here always...'

In Mortuary Lane a gull
cried on one of the Hospital gutters
I.I.I... harsh in sadness
on and on, beak and gullet
open against the blue.

Darkness poured down indoors
through a half light stale as the grave
over plates and silver bowls
glimmering on a side table.

Down at the corner a flicker of sex
— a white dress — against the railings.

'This is where George Moore...'
                                        rasps
his phantom walking stick
without a sound, toward the Post Office
where her slight body, in white, has disappeared.

A blood vision started out of the brick:
a flustered perfumy dress;
a mothering shocked smile;
live muscle startling in skin.
The box of keys in my pocket
— I am opening it, tongue-tied.
I unpick the little penknife
and dig it in her throat,
in her spirting gullet.

And they are on it in a flash,
tongues of movement feeding,
ravenous and burrowing,
upstreaming through the sunlight with it
until it disappears, buried
in heaven, faint, far off.

'… with a wicked wit, but self-mocking;
and full of integrity behind it all…'

A few beginnings, a few
tentative tired endings
over and over.
                    Memoirs, maggots.
After lunch a quarter of an hour,
at most, of empty understanding.


## Worker in Mirror, at his Bench

### 1

Silent rapt surfaces
assemble glittering
among themselves.

A few more pieces
What to call it…
                    Bright Assembly?
Foundations for a Tower?
Open Trap? Circular-Tending
Self-Reflecting Abstraction…


### 2

The shop doorbell rings.
A few people enter.

I am sorry. You have caught me
a little early in my preparations.

The way they mess with everything.
Smile. How they tighten their lips:
What *is* it about the man
that is so impossible to like?
The flashy coat, the flourished cuffs?
The ease under questioning...

Yes, everything is deliberate.
This floppy flower. Smile.
This old cutaway style – all the easier
to bare the breast. Comfortable smiles.
A cheap lapse – forgive me;
the temptation never sleeps.
The smiles more watery.

No, it has no practical application.
I am simply trying to understand something
– states of peace nursed out of wreckage.
The peace of fullness, not emptiness.

It is tedious, yes. The process is elaborate,
and wasteful – a dangerous litter
of lacerating pieces collects.
Let my rubbish stand witness.
Smile, stirring it idly with a shoe.

Take for example this work in hand.
Out of its waste matter
it should emerge solid and light.
One idea, grown with the thing itself,
should drive it searching inward
with a sort of life, due to the mirror effect.
Often, the more I simplify
the more a few simplicities
go burrowing in their own depths
until the guardian structure is aroused.

Most satisfying, yes.
Another kind of vigour, I agree
– unhappy until its actions are more convulsed:
the 'passionate' – might find it maddening.
Here the passion is in the putting together.

Yes, I suppose I am appalled
at the massiveness of others' work.
But not deterred. I have leaned my shed
against a solid wall. Understanding smiles.
I tinker with the things that dominate me
as they describe their random persistent coherences.
Clean surfaces shift and glitter among themselves.

Pause. We all are vile...
Let the voice die away.

Awkward silence
as they make their way out.


3

But they are right to be suspicious
when answers distract and conceal.
What is there to understand?
Time punishes – and this the flesh teaches.
Emptiness, is that not peace?

Conceal and permit: pursuit
at its most delicate, truth as tinkering,
easing the particular of its litter,
bending attention on the remaining depths
as though questions had never been.


He bends closer, testing the work.
The bright assembly begins to turn in silence.
The answering brain glitters – one system
answering another. The senses enter
and reach out with a pulse of pleasure
to the four corners of their own wilderness:

A gold mask, vast in the distance, stares back.
Familiar features. Naked sky-blue eyes.
(It is morning, once upon a time.)
Disappears. Was it a dream? Forgotten.

Reappears: enormous and wavering. Silver.
Stern and beautiful, with something
not yet pain in the eyes.
The forehead begins to wrinkle:
what ancient sweet time… Forgotten.

Reestablishes: a bronze head
thrown back across the firmament,
a bronze arm covering the eyes.
Pain established. Eyes
that have seen… Forgotten.

Dark as iron. All the light
hammered into two blazing eyes;
all the darkness into one wolf-muzzle.
Resist! An unholy tongue
laps brothers' thick blood.
                              Forget!

He straightens up, unseeing.

Did I dream another outline
in the silt of the sea floor?
Blunt stump of limb – a marble carcass
where no living thing can have crept,
below the last darkness, slowly,
as the earth ages, blurring with pressure.
The calm smile of a half-buried face:
eyeball blank, the stare inward
to the four corners of
what foul continuum.

Blackness – all matter
in one polished cliff face
hurtling rigid from zenith to pit
through dead

# St Paul's Rocks: 16 February 1832

A cluster of rocks far from the trade routes,
a thousand miles from any other land,
they appear abruptly in the ocean,
low lying, so hidden in driving mists
they are seldom sighted, and then briefly,
white and glittering against the eternal grey.

Despite the lack of any vegetation
they have succeeded in establishing
symbiosis with the surrounding water.
Colonies of birds eat the abundant fish;
moths feed on the feathers; lice and beetles
live in the dung; countless spiders
prey on these scavengers; in the crevices
a race of crabs lives on the eggs and young.

In squalor and killing and parasitic things
life takes its first hold.
Later the noble accident: the seed,
dropped in some exhausted excrement,
or bobbing like a matted skull into an inlet.

# *Drowsing over* The Arabian Nights

I nodded. The books agree,
one hopes for too much.
It is ridiculous.
We are elaborate beasts.

If we concur it is only
in our hunger: the soiled gullet.
And sleep's airy nothing.
And the moist matter of lust

– if the whole waste of women
could be gathered like one pit
under swarming Man,
then all might act together.

And the agonies of death,
as we enter our endless nights
quickly, one by one, fire
darting up to the roots of our hair.

# Crab Orchard Sanctuary: Late October

The lake water lifted a little and fell
doped and dreamy in the late heat.
The air at lung temperature – like the end of the world:
a butterfly panted with dull scarlet wings
on the mud by the reeds, the tracks
of small animals softening along the edge,
a child's foot-prints, out too far.

The car park was empty. Long threads of spider silk
blew out softly from the tips of the trees.
A big spider stopped on the warm gravel,
sunlight charging the dark shell.

A naked Indian stepped out onto the grass
silent and savage, faded,
grew transparent, disappeared.

A speedboat glistened slowly in the distance.
A column of smoke climbed from the opposite shore.
In the far inlets clouds of geese flew about
quarrelling and settling in.

*

That morning
two thin quails appeared in our garden
stepping one by one with piping movements
across the grass, feeding. I watched a long time
until they rounded the corner of the house.
A few grey wasps still floated about at the eaves;
crickets still chirruped in the grass
– but in growing silence, after last week's frosts.
Now a few vacated bodies, locust wraiths,
light as dry scale, begin to drift
on the driveway among the leaves,
stiff little Fuseli devil bodies.
Hidden everywhere, a myriad
leather seed-cases lie in wait
nourishing curled worms of white fat

– ugly, in absolute certainty, piteous,
threatening in every rustling sound:
bushes worrying in the night breeze,
dry leaves detaching, and creeping.
They will swarm again, on suffocated nights,
with their endless hysterics; and wither away again.

*

Who will stand still then, listening
to that woodpecker knocking, and watch
the erratic jays and cardinals flashing
blue and red among the branches and trunks;
that bronze phantom pausing; and this…stock-still,
with glittering brain, withering away.

It is an ending already.
The road hot and empty, taken over
by spiders, and pairs of butterflies twirling
about one another, and grasshoppers leap-
drifting over the gravel, birds darting
fluttering through the heat.

What solitary step.

A slow hot glare out on the lake
spreading over the water.

# *Wyncote, Pennsylvania: a gloss*

A mocking-bird on a branch
outside the window, where I write,
gulps down a wet crimson berry,
shakes off a few bright drops
from his wing, and is gone
into a thundery sky.

Another storm coming.
Under that copper light
my papers seem luminous.
And over them I will take
ever more painstaking care.

# Peppercanister Poems

# A Selected Life

## (1972)

### 1 Galloping Green: May 1962

He clutched the shallow drum
and crouched forward, thin
as a beast of prey. The shirt
stretched at his waist. He stared
to one side, toward the others,
and struck the skin cruelly
with his nails. Sharp
as the answering arid bark
his head quivered, counting.

### 2 Coolea: 6 October 1971

A fine drizzle blew
softly across the tattered valley
onto my glasses, and covered
my mourning suit with tiny drops.

A crow scuffled in the hedge
and floated out with a dark groan
into full view. It flapped up the field
and lit on a rock, and scraped its beak.
It croaked: a voice out of the rock
carrying across the slope. Foretell.

Foretell: the Sullane river winding downward
in darker green through the fields
and disappearing behind his house;
cars parking in the lane; a bare yard;
family and friends collecting in the kitchen;
a shelf there, concertinas sprawled in the dust,
the pipes folded on their bag.
The hole waiting in the next valley.
That.

    A rat lay on its side in the wet,
the grey skin washed clean and fleshy,
the little face wrinkled back in hatred,
the back torn open. A pale string
stretched on the gravel. Devil-martyr:
your sad, mad meat.
                  I have interrupted
some thing…You! Croaking
on your wet stone. Flesh picker.

The drizzle came thick and fast suddenly.
Down in the village the funeral bell began to beat.

               *

And you. Waiting in the dark chapel.
Packed and ready. Upon your hour.
Leaving… A few essentials forgotten

– a standard array of dependent beings,
small, smaller, pale, paler, in black;

– sundry musical effects: a piercing
sweet consort of whistles crying,
goosenecked wail and yelp of pipes,
melodeons snoring in sadness,
drum bark, the stricken
harpsichord's soft crash;

– a lurid cabinet: fire's flames
plotting in the dark; hugger mugger
and murder; collapsing back in laughter.

Angry goblets of Ireland's tears,
stuffed with fire, touch. *Salut!*
Men's guts ignite and whiten in satisfaction;

– a workroom, askew: fumbling at the table
tittering, pools of idea forming.
A contralto fills the room
with Earth's autumnal angst; the pools coalesce.

Here and there in the shallows dim spirits
glide, poissons de la melancolie.
The banks above are smothered in roses;
among their glowing harmonies, bathed in charm,
a cavalier returns in fancy dress,
embracing her loving prize; two baby angels,
each holding a tasseled curtain-corner,
flutter down, clucking and mocking complacently.
Liquids of romance, babbling
on the concrete floor. Let us draw a veil.

### 3  St Gobnait's Graveyard, Ballyvourney: that evening

The gate creaked in the dusk. The trampled grass,
soaked and still, was disentangling
among the standing stones
after the day's excess.

A flock of crows circled
the church tower, scattered
and dissolved chattering
into the trees. Fed.

His first buried night
drew on. Unshuddering.
And welcome.
Shudder for him,

Pierrot limping forward in the sun
out of Merrion Square, long ago,
in black overcoat and beret,
pale as death from his soiled bed,

swallowed back: animus
brewed in clay, uttered
in brief meat and brains, flattened
back under our flowers.

Gold and still he lay,
on his secondlast bed. *Dottore!* A withered smile,
the wry hands lifted. *A little while
and you may not.*

*Salut.*
Slán.
*Yob tvoyu mat'.*
Master, your health.

# *Vertical Man*

## (1973)

### 4 Philadelphia: 3 October 1972

I was pouring a drink when the night-monotony
was startled below by a sudden howling
of engines along Market Street,
curséd ambulances intermixing their screams
down the dark canyons.

Over the gramophone your death-mask
was suddenly awake
and I felt something of you
out in the night, near and moving nearer,
tittering, uneasy.

I thought we had laid you to rest
– that you had been directed toward
crumbling silence, and the like.
It seems it is hard to keep
a vertical man down.

I lifted the glass, and the furies
redoubled their distant screams.
To you: the bourbon-breath.
To me, for the time being,
the real thing.

'There has grown lately upon the soul
a covering as of earth and stone,
thick and rough...'
                         I had been remembering
the sour ancient phrases...
                         'Very well,
seemingly the argument requires it:
let us assume mankind is worth considering...'
That particular heaviness.

                         That the days pass,
that our tasks arise, dominate our energies,
are mastered with difficulty and some pleasure,
and are obsolete. That there can be a sweet stir
hurrying in the veins (earned: this sunlight
– this oxygen – are my *reward*) and the ground
grows dull to the tread. The ugly rack: let it ride.
That you may startle the heart of a whole people
(as you know) and all your power,
with its delicate, self-mocking adjustments,
is soon beating to a coarse pulse
to glut fantasy and sentiment.
That for all you have done, the next beginning
is as lonely, as random, as gauche and unready,
as presumptuous, as the first,
when you stripped and advanced timidly
toward nothing in particular.
Though with a difference – there is
a kind of residue. Not an increase in weight
(we must not become portly; your admired Durrell,
the lush intellectual glamour loosening
to reveal the travelogue beneath).
But a residue in the timidity,
a maturer unsureness, as we
prepare to undergo preparatory error.

Only this morning...that desultory moment or two
standing at the rain-stained glass. A while more
looking over the charts pinned on the wall.
To sit down with the folder of notes on the left
and clean paper on the right, the pen beside it,
and remove and put down the spectacles and bury

my face in my hands, in self-devouring prayer,
till the charts and notes come crawling to life again
under a Night seething with
soft incandescent bombardment!

At the dark zenith a pulse beat,
a sperm of light separated
and snaked in a slow beam down
the curve of the sky, through faint
structures and hierarchies
of elements and things and beasts. It fell,
a packed star, dividing
and redividing until it was
a multiple gold tear. It dropped
toward the horizon, entered
bright Quincunx newly risen,
beat with a blinding flame and dis-
appeared.
                    I stared, duly blinded.
An image burned on the brain
– a woman-animal: scaled,
pierced in paws and heart,
ecstatically calm. It faded
to a far-off desolate call,
                    a child's.

If the eye could follow that, accustomed to
that dark.
                    But that is your domain.

At which thought, your presence
turned back toward the night.
                    (*Wohin...*)

But stay a while. Since you are here.
At least we have *Das Lied von der Erde*
and a decent record-player together
at the one place and time.

With a contraction of the flesh...
A year exactly since you died!

I arrested the needle. The room filled
with a great sigh.
                    In terror and memory
I lowered the tiny point toward our youth
– into those bright cascades!


                    Radiant outcry –
trumpets and drenching strings – exultant tenor –
*Schadenfreude!* The waste!
                    Abject. Irrecoverable.

Would you care to share a queer vision I had?
It was moonlight.
                    By your gravestone.
There was something crouching there – apeshaped –
demented, howling out
silent foulness, accursed silent screams
into the fragrant Night…


                    *

The golden bourbon trembled  in the glass.
For the road.
                    It was time.
And more than time.

He stepped forward, through the cigarette smoke,
to his place at the piano
– all irritation – and tore off
his long fingernails to play.

From palatal darkness a voice
rose flickering, and checked
in glottal silence. The song
articulated and pierced.

We leaned over the shallows from the boat slip
and netted the little grey shrimp-ghosts
snapping, and dropped them
in the crawling biscuit-tin.

from

# *One*

(1974)

## *Finistère*

1
One.

I smelt the weird Atlantic.
Finistère…
                    Finisterre…

The sea surface darkened. The land behind me,
and all its cells and cists, grew dark.
From a bald boulder on the cairn top
I spied out the horizon to the northwest
and sensed that minute imperfection again.
Where the last sunken ray withdrew.
A point of light.

A maggot of the possible
wriggled out of the spine
into the brain.

We hesitated before that wider sea
but our heads sang with purpose
and predatory peace.

And whose excited blood was that
fumbling our movements? Whose ghostly hunger
tunnelling our thoughts full of passages
smelling of death and clay and faint metals
and great stones in the darkness?

At no great distance out in the bay
the swell took us into its mercy,
grey upheaving slopes of water
sliding under us, collapsing,
crawling onward, mountainous.

Driven outward a day and a night
we held fast, numbed by the steady
might of the oceanic wind.
We drew close together, as one,
and turned inward, salt chaos
rolling in silence all around us,
and listened to our own mouths
mumbling in the sting of spray:

       – Ill wind end well
       mild mother
       on wild water pour peace

       who gave us our unrest
       whom we meet and unmeet
       in whose yearning shadow
       we erect our great uprights
       and settle fulfilled
       and build and are still
       unsettled, whose goggle gaze
       and holy howl we have scraped
       speechless on slabs of stone
       poolspirals opening on
       closing spiralpools
       and dances drilled in the rock
       in coil zigzag angle and curl
       river ripple earth ramp
       suncircle moonloop…
       in whose outflung service
       we nourished our hunger
       uprooted and came
       in whale hell
                gale gullet
      salt hole
           dark nowhere
      calm queen
           pour peace

The bad dream ended at last.
In the morning, in a sunny breeze,
bare headlands rose fresh out of the waves.
We entered a deep bay, lying open
to all the currents of the ocean.
We were further than anyone had ever been
and light-headed with exhaustion and relief
– three times we misjudged and were nearly driven
on the same rock.
                    (I had felt all this before.)
We steered in along a wall of mountain
and entered a quiet hall of rock echoing
to the wave-wash and our low voices.
I stood at the prow. We edged to a slope of stone.

I steadied myself. 'Our Father...' someone said
and there was a little laughter. I stood
searching a moment for the right words.
They fell silent. I chose the old words once more
and stepped out. At the solid shock
a dreamy power loosened at the base of my spine
and uncoiled and slid up through the marrow.
A flow of seawater over the rock fell back
with a she-hiss, plucking at my heel.
My tongue stumbled

Who
        is a breath
that makes the wind
that makes the wave
that makes   this   voice?

Who
        is the bull with seven scars
the hawk on the cliff
the salmon sunk in his pool
the pool sunk in her soil
the animal's fury
the flower's fibre
a teardrop in the sun?

Who
        is the word that spoken
the spear springs
        and pours out terror
the spark springs
        and burns in the brain?

When men meet on the hill
dumb as stones in the dark
        (the craft knocked behind me)
who is the jack of all light?
Who goes in full into
the moon's interesting conditions?
Who fingers the sun's sink hole:
        (I went forward, reaching out)


## 38 Phoenix Street

Look.
        I was lifted up
past rotten bricks weeds
to look over the wall.
A mammy lifted up a baby on the other side.
Dusty smells. Cat. Flower bells
hanging down purple red.

Look.
        The other. Looking.
My finger picked at a bit of dirt
on top of the wall and a quick
wiry redgolden thing
ran back down a little hole.

*

We knelt up on our chairs in the lamplight
and leaned on the brown plush, watching the gramophone.
The turning record shone and hissed
under the needle, liftfalling, liftfalling.
John McCormack chattered in his box.

Two little tongues of flame burned
in the lamp chimney, wavering
their tips. On the glass belly
little drawnout images quivered.
Jimmy's mammy was drying the delph in the shadows.

*

Mister Cummins always hunched down
sad and still beside the stove,
with his face turned away toward the bars.
His mouth so calm, and always set so sadly.
A black rubbery scar stuck on his white forehead.

Sealed in his sad cave. Hisshorror erecting
slowly out of its rock nests, nosing the air.
He was buried for three days under a hill of dead,
the faces congested down all round him
grinning *Dardanelles!* in the dark.

They noticed him by a thread of blood
glistening among the black crusts on his forehead.
His heart gathered all its weakness, to beat.

A worm hanging down, its little round
black mouth open. Sad father.

*

I spent the night there once
in a strange room, tucked in against the wallpaper
on the other side of our own bedroom wall.

Up in the corner of the darkness the Sacred Heart
leaned down in his long clothes over a red oil lamp
with his women's black hair and his eyes lit up in red,
hurt and blaming. He held out the Heart
with his women's fingers, like a toy.

The lamp-wick, with a tiny head
of red fire, wriggled in its pool.
The shadows flickered: the Heart beat!

# Minstrel

He trailed a zither from
melancholy pale fingers, sighing.
A mist of tears lay still upon the land.

The fire burned down in the grate.
A light burned on the bare ceiling.
A dry teacup stained the oil cloth
where I wrote, bent like a feeding thing
over my own source.

A spoonful of white ash fell
with a soundless puff, undetected.
A shadow, or the chill of night,
advanced out of the corner.
I stopped, my hand lifted
an inch from the page.

Outside, the heavens listened,
a starless diaphragm
stopped miles overhead
to hear the remotest whisper
of returning matter, missing
an enormous black beat.

The earth stretched out in answer.
Little directionless instincts
uncoiled from the wet mud-cracks,
crept in wisps of purpose, and vanished
leaving momentary traces        .
of claw marks, breasts,
ribs, feathery prints,

eyes shutting and opening
all over the surface.
A distant point of light
winked at the edge of nothing.

A knock on the window
and everything in fantasy fright
flurried and disappeared.
My father looked in from the dark,
my face black-mirrored beside his.

## His Father's Hands

I drank firmly
and set the glass down between us firmly.
You were saying.

My father.
Was saying.

His finger prodded and prodded,
marring his point. Emphas-
emphasemphasis.

I have watched
his father's hands before him

cupped, and tightening the black Plug
between knife and thumb,
carving off little curlicues
to rub them in the dark of his palms,

or cutting into new leather at his bench,
levering a groove open with his thumb,
insinuating wet sprigs for the hammer.

He kept the sprigs in mouthfuls
and brought them out in silvery
units between his lips.

I took a pinch out of their hole
and knocked them one by one into the wood,
bright points among hundreds gone black,
other children's – cousins and others, grown up.

Or his bow hand scarcely moving,
scraping in the dark corner near the fire,
his plump fingers shifting on the strings.

To his deaf, inclined head
he hugged the fiddle's body
whispering with the tune

with breaking heart
whene'er I hear
in privacy, across a blocked void,

the wind that shakes the barley.
The wind...
round her grave...

on my breast in blood she died...
But blood for blood without remorse
I've ta'en...

Beyond that.

*

Your family, Thomas, met with and helped
many of the Croppies in hiding from the Yeos
or on their way home after the defeat
in south Wexford. They sheltered the Laceys
who were later hanged on the Bridge in Ballinglen
between Tinahely and Anacorra.

From hearsay, as far as I can tell
the Men Folk were either Stone Cutters
or masons or probably both.
                                    In the 18
and late 1700s even the farmers
had some other trade to make a living.

They lived in Farnese among a Colony
of North of Ireland or Scotch settlers left there
in some of the dispersals or migrations
which occurred in this Area of Wicklow and Wexford
and Carlow. And some years before that time
the Family came from somewhere around Tullow.

Beyond that.

                                    *


Littered uplands. Dense grass. Rocks everywhere,
wet underneath, retaining memory of the long cold.

First, a prow of land
chosen, and webbed with tracks;
then boulders chosen
and sloped together, stabilized in menace.

I do not like this place.
I do not think the people who lived here
were ever happy. It feels evil.
Terrible things happened.
I feel afraid here when I am on my own.

                                    *

Dispersals or migrations.
Through what evolutions or accidents
toward that peace and patience
by the fireside, that blocked gentleness...

That serene pause, with the slashing knife,
in kindly mockery,
as I busy myself with my little nails
at the rude block, his bench.

The blood advancing
– gorging vessel after vessel –
and altering in them
one by one.

Behold, that gentleness already
modulated twice, in others:
to earnestness and iteration;
to an offhandedness, repressing various impulses.

\*

Extraordinary... The big block – I found it
years afterward in a corner of the yard
in sunlight after rain
and stood it up, wet and black:
it turned under my hands, an axis
of light flashing down its length,
and the wood's soft flesh broke open,
countless little nails
squirming and dropping out of it.

# Epilogue

*The great cell of nightmare rose in pallor*
*and shed its glare down on the calm gulf.*

*A woman waited at the edge, with lank hair.*
*She spread it out. It stiffened and moved*
*by itself, glistening on her shoulders.*

*We squirmed in expectation. Then there rose*
*a suffused heart, stopped, clenched on its light.*
*'Reap us!' we hissed, in praise. The heart beat*
*and broke open, and sent a fierce beam*
*among our wriggling sheaves.*

*Caught in her cold fist, I writhed and reversed.*

*

*Mostly the thing runs smoothly, the fall is cradled*
*immediately in a motherly warmth, with nothing*
*to disturb the dark urge, except from within*
*– a tenseness, as it coils on itself, changing*
*to obscure substance.*

*Anxieties pass through it,*
*but it can make no sense of them. It knows*
*only that it is nightmare-bearing tissue*
*and that there are others. They drift together*
*through 'incommunicable' dark, one by one,*

*toward the dawn zone, not knowing or caring*
*that they share anything.*
                    *Awakening,*
*their ghost-companionship dissolves back*
*into private shadow, not often called upon.*

from

# A Technical Supplement

## (1976)

*My dear master, I am over forty. I am tired out with tricks and shufflings. I cry from morning till night for rest, rest; and scarcely a day passes when I am not tempted to go and live in obscurity and die in peace in the depths of my old country. There comes a time when all ashes are mingled. Then what will it boot me to have been Voltaire or Diderot, or whether it is your three syllables or my three syllables that survive? One must work, one must be useful, one owes an account of one's gifts, etcetera, etcetera. Be useful to men! Is it quite clear that one does more than amuse them, and that there is much difference between the philosopher and the flute-player? They listen to one and the other with pleasure or disdain, and remain what they were. The Athenians were never wickeder than in the time of Socrates, and perhaps all they owe to his existence is a crime the more. That there is more spleen than good sense in all this, I admit – and back to the Encylopaedia I go.*

Diderot to Voltaire, 19 February 1758, *trans.* John Viscount Morley

## 11

The shower is over.
And there's the sun out again
and the sound of water outside
trickling clean into the shore.
And the little washed bird–chirps and trills.

A watered peace. Drop. At the heart.
Drop. The unlikely heart.

A shadow an instant
on the window. A bird.
And the sun is gone in again.

(Good withdrawn, that other good may come.)

We have shaped and polished.
We have put a little darkness behind us,
we are out of that soup.
Into a little brightness.
That soup.

The mind flexes.
The heart encloses.


## 12


It might be just as well not to worry too much
about our other friend.

He was mainly captious and fanciful.
Gifted, certainly, but finally he leaves
a shrug of disappointment.
Good company from time to time
but it was best kept offhand.
Any regularity, any intimacy,
and the veneer … Mean as a cat,
always edging for the small advantage.

But he *could* compete.
There isn't a day passes but I thank God
some others I know – I can see them, mounting up
with grim pleasure to the judgement seat –
didn't 'fulfil their promise'.

An arrogant beginning, *then*
the hard attrition.
                    Stomach that
and you find a kind of strength not to be had
any other way. Enforced humility,

*with* all the faculties. Making for
a small excellence – very valuable.

There, at the unrewarding outer reaches,
the integrity of the whole thing is tested.


## 13

Hand lifted. Song.
     I hear.
Hand on breast. Dear heart.
      I know.
Hand at the throat. Funnelled blood.
        It is yours.
Hand over eyes. I see.
     I see.


## 14

My eye hurt. I lay down
and pressed it shut into
the palm of my hand.

I slept uneasily
  *a dish of ripe eyes gaped up*
  *at the groaning iron press descending*
   and dreamed
I pulled a sheet of brilliant colour
free from the dark.

## 15

The pen writhed. It moved
under my thumb!
          It has sensed
that sad prowler on our landing again.

If she dares come nearer, if she dares…
She and her 'sudden and
peremptory incursions'…
I'll pierce her like
a soft fruit, a soft big seed!


## 21

The residue of a person's work.

The words 'water' or 'root'
offered in real refreshment. The words
'Love', 'Truth', etc., offered with force
but self-serving, therefore ineffective.
A fading pose – the lonely prowl of the outcast.

Or half a dozen outward howls of glory
and noble despair. Borrowed glory,
his own despair. For the rest, energy wasted
grimacing facetiously inward. And yet
a vivid and lasting image: the racked outcast.

Or opinion modified or sharpened, in search.
Emotion expelled, to free the structure of a thing,
or indulged, to free the structure of an idea.
The entirety of one's being
crowded for everlasting shelter
into the memory of one crust of bread.
Granting it everlasting life.
Eating it absolutely.

Somehow it all matters ever after – very much –
though each little thing matters little
however painful that may be.

And remember that foolishness
though it may give access to heights of vision
in certain gifted abnormal brains
remains always what it is.


## 24

It is time I continued my fall.

The divider waits, shaped
razor sharp to my dream print.

I should feel nothing.

Turning slowly and more slowly
we drifted to rest in a warmth of flesh,
twinned, glaring and growing.

from

# Song of the Night and Other Poems

(1978)

## Artists' Letters

Folders, papers, proofs, maps
with tissue paper marked and coloured.
I was looking for something,
confirmation of something,
in the cardboard box
when my fingers deflected among
fat packets of love letters,
old immediacies in elastic bands.

I shook a letter open from
its creases, carefully, and read
– and shrugged, embarrassed.
                      Then stirred.
My hand grew thin and agitated
as the words crawled again
quickly over the dried paper.

Letter by letter the foolishness
deepened, but displayed
a courage in its own unsureness;
acknowledged futility and waste
in all their importance ... a young idiocy
in desperate full-hearted abandon
to all the chance of one choice:

There is one throw, no more. One
offering: make it. With no style
– these are desperate times. There is
a poverty of spirit in the wind;
a shabby richness in braving it.
My apologies, but you are my beloved
and I will not be put off.

What is it about such letters,
torn free ignominiously
in love? Character stripped off,
our pens plunge repeatedly
at the unique cliché, cover
ache after ache of radiant paper
with analytic ecstasies,
wrestle in repetitious fury.

The flesh storms our brain; we storm
our entranced opposite, badger her
with body metaphors, project
our selves with out-thrust stuttering arms,
cajoling, forcing her
– her spread-eagled spirit –
to accept our suspect cries
with shocked and shining eyes.

Artists' letters (as the young career
grows firmer in excited pride
and moves toward authority
after the first facetiousness,
the spirit shaken into strength
by shock after shock of understanding)
suddenly shudder and *display*! Animal.
Violent vital organs of desire.

A toothless mouth opens
and we throw ourselves, enthralled, against our bonds
and thrash toward her. And when we have
been nicely eaten and our parts
spat out whole and have became
'one', *then* we can settle our cuffs
and our Germanic collar
and turn back calmly toward distinguished things.

# Tao and Unfitness at Inistiogue on the River Nore

## Noon

The black flies kept nagging in the heat.
Swarms of them, at every step, snarled
off pats of cow dung spattered in the grass.

Move, if you move, like water.

The punts were knocking by the boathouse, at full tide.
Volumes of water turned the river curve
hushed under an insect haze.

Slips of white,
trout bellies, flicked in the corner of the eye
and dropped back onto the deep mirror.

Respond. Do not interfere. Echo.

Thick green woods along the opposite bank
climbed up from a root-dark recess
eaved with mud-whitened leaves.

*

In a matter of hours all that water is gone,
except for a channel near the far side.
Muck and shingle and pools where the children
wade, stabbing flatfish.

## Afternoon

Inistiogue itself is perfectly lovely,
like a typical English village, but a bit sullen.
Our voices echoed in sunny corners
among the old houses; we admired
the stonework and gateways, the interplay
of roofs and angled streets.

The square, with its 'village green', lay empty.
The little shops had hardly anything.
The Protestant church was guarded by a woman
of about forty, a retainer, spastic
and indistinct, who drove us out.

An obelisk to the Brownsfoords and a Victorian
Celto-Gothic drinking fountain, erected
by a Tighe widow for the villagers,
'erected' in the centre. An astronomical-looking
sundial stood sentry on a platform
on the corner where High Street went up out of the square.

We drove up, past a long-handled water pump
placed at the turn, with an eye to the effect,
then out of the town for a quarter of a mile
above the valley, and came to the dead gate
of Woodstock, once home of the Tighes.

                              *


The great ruin presented its flat front
at us, sunstruck. The children disappeared.
Eleanor picked her way around a big fallen branch
and away along the face toward the outbuildings.
I took the grassy front steps and was gathered up
in a brick-red stillness. A rook clattered out of the dining room.

A sapling, hooked thirty feet up
in a cracked corner, held out a ghost-green
cirrus of leaves. Cavities
of collapsed fireplaces connected silently
about the walls. Deserted spaces, complicated
by door-openings everywhere.

There was a path up among bushes and nettles
over the beaten debris, then a drop, where bricks
and plaster and rafters had fallen into the kitchens.
A line of small choked arches... The pantries, possibly.

Be still, as though pure.

A brick, and its dust, fell.

# Nightfall

The trees we drove under in the dusk
as we threaded back along the river through the woods
were no mere dark growth, but a flitting-place
for ragged feeling, old angers and rumours.

Black and Tan ghosts up there, at home
on the Woodstock heights: an iron mouth
scanning the Kilkenny road: the house
gutted by the townspeople and burned to ruins.

The little Ford we met, and inched past, full of men
we had noticed along the river bank during the week,
disappeared behind us into a fifty-year-old night.
Even their caps and raincoats...

Sons, or grandsons. Poachers.
                              Mud-tasted salmon
slithering in a plastic bag around the boot,
bloodied muscle, disputed since King John.

The ghosts of daughters of the family
waited in the uncut grass as we drove
down to our mock-Austrian lodge and stopped.

*

We untied the punt in the half-light, and pushed out
to take a last hour on the river, until night.
We drifted, but stayed almost still.
The current underneath us
and the tide coming back to the full
cancelled in a gleaming calm, punctuated
by the plop of fish.

Down on the water... at eye level... in the little light
remaining overhead...the mayfly passed in a loose drift,
thick and frail, a hatch slow with sex,
separate morsels trailing their slack filaments,
olive, pale evening dun, imagoes, unseen eggs
dropping from the air, subimagoes, the river filled
with their nymphs ascending and excited trout.

Be subtle, as though not there.

We were near the island – no more than a dark mass
on a sheet of silver – when a man appeared in mid-river
quickly and with scarcely a sound, his paddle touching
left and right of the prow, with a sack behind him.
The flat cot's long body slid past effortless
as a fish, sinewing from side to side,
as he passed us and vanished.

## *Song of the Night*

### Philadelphia

A compound bass roar
an ocean voice
Metropolis in the ear
soft-thundered among the towers below
breaking in a hiss of detail
but without wave-rhythm
without breath-rhythm
exhalation without cease
amplified
of terrible pressure
interrupted by brief blasts and nasal shouts
guttural diesels
a sky-train waning in a line of thunder.

I opened the great atlas on the desk.

The Atlantic curved on the world.

### Carraroe

Our far boundary was Gorumna island
low on the water, dotted
with granite erratics, extended grey-green
along the opposite shore of the bay
toward the south Connemara series.

On our shore, among a tumble of boulders
on the minced coral, there was one
balanced with rugged edge upward,
stuck with limpets. Over it,
with the incoming tide, the waters

wash back and forth irregularly
and cover and uncover the brown angles.
Films of liquid light run
shimmering, cut by shell-points, over
stone inclines and clotted buds of anemones.

The films fatten with plasm and flow and fill
more loosely over the rock and gradually drown it.
Then larger movements invade from further out,
from the depths,
alive and in movement. At night-time,

in the wind, at that place,
the water-wash lapped at itself under the rocks
and withdrew rustling down the invisible grains.
The ocean worked in dark masses in the bay
and applied long leverage at the shore.

\*

We were finished, and quiet.
The music was over.
The lamp hissed in the tent.

We collected the cooking things
and plates and mugs and cutlery
scattered around us in the grass,
everything bone cold,
and put it all in the basin.

I unhooked the lamp and made my way down
flickering over the rocks with the children
to the edge of the ocean.

A cell of light hollowed around us
out of the night. Splashes and clear voices echoed
as the spoons and knives were dug down
and enamel plates scooped under water
into the sand, and scraped and rinsed.

I held the lamp out a little over the sea.
Silvery sand-eels seethed everywhere we stepped:
shivered and panicked through the shallows,
vanished – became sand – were discovered,
picked up with exclamations,
held out damp and deathly,
little whips fainted away
in wet small palms, in an iodine smell.

*

She was standing in a sheltered angle,
urgent and quiet.
                    'Look back.'

The great theatre of Connemara,
dark. A cloud bank stretched in folds
across the sky, luminous
with inner activity.

Centred on the beached lamp
a single cell of cold light
– part land and part living water –
blazed with child voices.

They splashed about the stark red basin,
pouncing. They lifted it and consulted.
Their crystalline laughter escaped upward,
their shadows huge.

*

We made off toward the rocky point
past the tent's walls flapping.

A new music came on the wind: string sounds hissing
mixed with a soft inner-ear roar
blown off the ocean; a persistent
tympanum double-beat ('...darkly expressive,
coming from innermost depths...') That old
body music. *Schattenhaft*. SONG OF THE NIGHT.
A long horn call, 'a single note
that lingers, changing colour as it fades...'

Overhead a curlew responded.
'poignant...' Yes.
'hauntingly beautiful...' Yes!

The bay – every inlet – lifted
and glittered toward us in articulated light.
The land, a pitch-black stage
of boulder shapes and scalps of heaped weed,
inhaled.

        A part of the mass
grated and tore, cranking harshly,
and detached and struggled upward
and beat past us along the rocks,
bat-black, heron-slow.

from

# Songs of the Psyche

## (1985)

## from *Songs of the Psyche*

### 6

I have kissed the inner earth
and the grin of stone upon stone
and it was time again

to surrender
to your
beaten smile

### 7

And she came by a little-haunted path
with modest run advancing
dancing in her flowers
awkwardly up to me.

It was something
to take a little of the spring
out of a person's step.
She offered me her hands.

I took them in mine
— averse
            but it was enough:
we were no longer two

but a third
            fumbling
ghost at polite ghost
of its own matter.


8


A tree with a twisted trunk;
two trees grown into one.
A heart-carving grown thick,
the cuts so deep.

The leaves reached out past us
and hissed: *We were so fond of you!*
There was a stir of flower heads
about our feet

gold for the first blaze,
red for the rough response,
dark blue for misunderstanding,
jet black for rue,

pale for the
unfinished children
that are
waiting everywhere

## 11

Come with me
    o'er the crystal stream
where eyelids dart
    in the dappled shallows

to where you wait
    on the farther bank
troubled and pretty
    with tattered basket.

Your feathery flesh
    I will kneel and kiss.
Your slender bones
    I will take in mine.

I will pick a straw
    from your stiffened dress
and so retire
    while the grasses whisper

and leeches wrinkle
    black in the water,
willow leaves
    that have fed on blood.

# from *Notes*

## Self-Scrutiny

The threadbare body gathers
with a new consideration
about the hidden bones
that shimmered once like spears
of iris in the mind.
It grows conscious
of its composite parts:

the eyes wet with delicacy
that will yet close
under unopenable marble;

the ear admitting the snarl
of mutabilitie
direct to the brain;

the tongue clung more with understanding
to the roof of the mouth
the more it is loosed in the savour of freedom
or the curse made flesh;

the thumbs and digits
pressed into the temples
at the felt limit of our range.

## Self-Release

Possibly you would rather I stopped
– uttering guttural Christ curses
and destroying my nails down the wall
or dashing myself to pieces once and for all
in a fury beside your head?

I will ease it somehow.
I could pull down a clean knife-shaft
two-handed into the brain and worry it
minutely about until there is
glaze and numbness in 'that' area.

Then you would see how charming
it is possible to be,
how fluent and fascinating,
a startlement to all,
internationally, and beyond.

## Self-Renewal

Reverently I swung open
the two side mirrors to reveal
everywhere, on a white brow crossed,
two ragged cuts; a wet mouth
held shut; eyes hurt and full.

I peered into these
and their velvet stirred
with the pale secrets of all
the lonely that had ever sat
by their lonely mirrors

studying the shame
that had brought them to sit there
and kiss the icy glass
and recover themselves a little

with icy brow on brow,
and one eye cocked at itself,
until they felt more able
to slip off about their business

with the glass clouding over
a couple of fading eye diagrams.

from

# Out of Ireland

(1987)

## *Harmonies*

Seamus of the Smart Suit, box player,
made signals to us across the grass tussocks and graves
the day we all came down from Cork
to commemorate our musical friend.

By Gobnait's sculpted lump
– a slab of a woman on a frieze of stone buds
and the locked bodies of bees –
he struggled in his nose with English,

showing the Holy Stations and instructing
with rigid finger and embarrassed snorts,
his box squeezed shut back in the house
with Mairtín's pipes and the pair of fiddles,

the same instruments, ranging together
in natural sweetness, with a many-sounded
and single voice, that gave Iohannes Scotus
– Eriugena, and instructing the known world –

his harmonious certainty: that the world's parts,
ill-fitted in their stresses and their pains,
will combine at last in polyphonic sweet-breathing union
and all created Nature ascend like joined angels,

limbs and bodies departing the touch of Earth
static in a dance of return, all Mankind
gathered stunned at the world's edge
silent in a choir of understanding.

## The Dance

It is the staling music of memory
has brought us nosing once more
around our forgotten young hero

and his high-spirited doings.
Grieving solos fade
and twine on echoes of each other

down the shallow valley:
his own voices,
divided against themselves.

His spirit, in one piece still
(just for a little while,
and only just)

is cavorting in answer
all brains and bare feet
along the scruffy skyline,

stepping the parish boundary
in goodbye
and beckoning with a comical thumb

up over the edge:
*Come and buy*
*my terrible new capabilities...*

The little plants shivering
green and pale on the far slope
in a breeze out of the Next Testament,

unplaceable, familiar smells
stealing among the goats'
dainty, unbothered feet.

And there would be no sign
if we tried to follow
his shifting rhythms,

the throaty piping,
the dry taps fractured on the drum skin,
the delicate new hooves

on approval, slithering to the beat
down out of sight
into the stony places.

# *Exit*

Lidless, lipless, opensocketed
and dumb with suspended understanding,
waiting for the Day,

our own best evidence
is aligned all about under us,
their figures finished.

The dance is at our feet.
    *Tabhair dom do lámh.*
               A careful step

together over that outstuck
tongue, and shut this gate
in God's name

behind us, once and for all.
And reach me my weapon
in the goat-grey light.

from

# *Personal Places*

### (1990)

There are established personal places
that receive our lives' heat
and adapt in their mass, like stone.

These absorb in their changes
the radiance of change in us,
and give it back

to the darkness of our understanding,
directionless
into the returning cold.


## *Brothers in the Craft*

In the creative generations there is often
a conspiracy of the mature and the brilliant young;
a taking in hand, in hopes of a handing on.

In the elder, an impulse against that settled state
when the elements work in balance against each other
in worn stability, no longer questioned;

to borrow something out of the restlessnesses
of the half ready, confide an ethereal itch
into new, committed fingers.

                              In the other,
a self-elect asking only to watch
– even be let hold something – the imbalance of growth.

These settle in the medium in their turn,
a part of the lasting colour of the work
taken from the early accidental particulars.


Again and again, in the Fifties, 'we' attended
Austin Clarke. He murmured in mild malice
and directed his knife-glance curiously amongst us.

Out in the dark, on a tree branch near the Bridge,
the animus of Yeats perched.
                              Another part of the City,
Tonio Kroeger, malodorous, prowled Inchicore.




## In Memory

### 1

You were silver-quiffed and tall
and smiling above us in public,
formal and at ease. Established.
Introducing I have forgotten what.

It is you I remember.
Authoritative, from the Department.
Published recently, and discussed.
Managing both careers.

The audience, mainly literary,
stood about, interested
in what was to come. But we
were gathered at your feet.

## 2

The years passed. Our group broke up.
The character of our generation
emerged, with the fulfilment
and the failure of early promise,

with achievement in surprising places,
and one startling success
revealing a sagacity and a scope
undreamed of at the time.

Some left the country, or disappeared
as though they had never been.
Others stayed in irregular contact
our conversations growing more general.


## 3

A few assembled lately
on a miserable occasion.
We found each other in a crowd
from the intervening years,

familiar and unfamiliar faces,
acquaintances and strangers,
friends from later interests.
An unpleasantness here and there

– one, quiet-spoken and confiding,
not to be trusted again;
one nursing an old dispute
and able behind the scenes.

The narrow face of envy.
Hardness of heart. Self.
False witness. The irreducible
malice and greed of the species.

*

We stood near the older trees
– your box, massive and pale,
waiting on a pile of clay.
With what you were taking with you.

And leaving. The memory
of a gentle self, affronted
by the unmanageable,
aroused and self-devouring.


I walked away, along a file
of long-established graves,
remembering our last meeting.
You, overcoated and withdrawn,

sitting beside the fire
after another death.
Violent. One of yours,
inheriting your luck.

And I, making my way across
and settling at your side.
You starting a conversation
out of another time.


When I turned around to go back
it was a while before I discovered
our people among the others
– everybody everywhere with white hair.

# Dura Mater

## 1

A potato smell came out from the kitchen door,
and a saucepan smell, with a piece of beef boiling.

She came along the passage in her slippers
with a fuzz of navy hair, and her long nails
held out wet out of the washing water.

Come here to me. Come here to me, my own son.

Stiff necked, she put up her pursed mouth
at her grown young – whatever idea she had of it
in behind the ill temper in her eyes.

Will you look at him. How do you stick him at all.

And offered, and withdrew, a Cupid's Bow
puckered; closed lids; a cheek of withered silk;
the little smell of her hairline powdered over.

## 2

The withheld kiss returned
onto her stone forehead. Dura Mater.

To take it, a seal on her stone will,
in under the screwed lid.

# At the Western Ocean's Edge

Hero as liberator. There is also
the warrior marked by Fate, who overmasters
every enemy in the known world
until the elements reveal themselves.
And one, finding the foe inside his head,
who turned the struggle outward, against the sea.

Yeats discovered him through Lady Gregory,
and found him helpful as a second shadow
in his own sour duel with the middle classes.
He grew to know him well in his own right
– mental strife; renewal in reverse;
emotional response; the revelation.


Aogan O Rathaille felt their forces meeting
at the Western ocean's edge
– the energy of chaos and a shaping
counter-energy in throes of balance;
the gale wailing inland off the water
arousing a voice responding in his head,

storming back at the waves with their own force
in a posture of refusal, beggar rags
in tatters in a tempest of particulars.
A battered figure. Setting his face
beyond the ninth shadow, into dead calm.
The stranger waiting on the steel horizon.

from

# Poems from Centre City

## (1990)

### Administrator

We knew him first as a pious reputation,
businesslike, a new breed in the neighbourhood.
Stationed out among the people. Accustomed
to property and its management. Seldom seen.

He appeared once, in response to a complaint.
Entered the front hall, quietly discourteous,
suited in grey, easy to mistake
for a Protestant colleague;
and sat across the table, not really listening,
his response ready, looking past the speaker.

Our charges have certain needs. If these entail
annoyance for others that is unfortunate.
But we are there.
                    One lapse: a fumbled exit.

Then handed matters back to the lay staff.

# Social Work

The meeting ended, and the delegates
moved off among themselves around the room.
I turned away to talk to a new neighbour.

A voice at my ear: 'I think we may give it up.'
A pair of furious Corporation officials
had stepped across to one of the high windows

with the social workers – the very Catholic doctor,
the house agent at his elbow, silver-haired –
and the parish priest, present as an observer.

The latter had chatted pleasantly before the meeting
but was otherwise quiet. He was speaking now
at the centre of the group, the others nodding.

# The Stranger

Years ago, while we were settling in,
I saw him passing by this side of the Canal,
a clerk from somewhere in the area.

Then, more accustomed to the neighbourhood,
I noticed him the other side of the Bridge,
crossing over from Mount Street opposite

or turning away in the dark along the base
of the heavy-set terrace, back around the Church
with the little peppercanister cupola.

One evening, when our house was full of neighbours
met in upset, I was standing by the drapes
and saw his face outside, turned up to the light.

And once in Baggot Street I was talking with someone
when he passed with a word or two to the other, his face
arab up close. We smiled in antipathy.


In another time I might have put it down
to evil luck or early death – the Stranger
close upon our heels – and taken care.

But you and I were starting to deal already
with troubles any Stranger might desire.
Our minds in their teeming patterns died each night.


Once, at an upper window, at my desk,
with the photographs and cuttings pinned in fury
around the wall, and tacked across the blind,

I found a structure for my mess of angers,
lifted out of the school dark:
                              Distracted

one morning by a stream, in circumstances
of loveliness and quiet, not for him,
a poet sinks to the ground and hides his face

in harrowed sleep. A kindly beauty approaches,
unworldly, but familiar – one of us –
comforts his misery, and turns his thoughts

toward some theatrical hope...
                              He reawakens,
distracted still.

A simple form; adjusting
simply with the situation,
and open to local application; weakened

by repetition; ridiculed and renewed
at last in parody. My pen quickened
in a pulse of doggerel ease.

When I beheld him the other side of the road,
overacting, bowing with respect;
resuming his night patrol along the terrace.

Leaving my fingers stopped above the paper.


## The Last

Standing stone still on the path, with long pale chin
        under a broad-brimmed hat, and aged eyes
staring down Baggot Street across his stick.
        Jack Yeats. The last.

Upright, stately and blind, and hesitating
        solitary on the lavatory floor
after the Government meeting down the hall.
        De Valera. The last.

# Memory of W.H. Auden

A tangle of concerns
above the dark channel of Baggot Street.
Jesus in History. Man and his Symbols.
Civilisation Surprised in her Underwear.

At a loss. At my upper window.
Looking out at nothing.
My scribal claws picking at the paint.

When I felt a stone-bright dead light
move on their pallor.
Not an earthly effect. But not imagined
– the chimneys and the slate roofs South to the hills
touched by the same.

                      Corpsegaze. Swollen full on high.
Ghost of brilliance, staring down out of the Thirties
– rapt, radiant with vision and opinion.
Battered with the final furrows.

*

I turned back to my den,
the scarred regard bright over my shoulder.
My fingers, with the taint upon them,
finding their way back about their business.

from

# Madonna and Other Poems

(1991)

## Madonna

Her high heels sounded nearer
in the aisle, tapping on the tiles.

She knelt beside me at the money-box
in the light of the candles,
under the Body with the woman feet.

Her head bowed. Her meat sweet.

\*

She was busy, minding her hair
at the window, a long brushful held out.

Looking out at the night
and the light coming in
dead white off the street, and the shadow
invading our urinary privacy.

\*

In concern and familiarity
it is done: our two awarenesses
narrowed into one point,
our piercing presences exchanged
in pleasantry and fright.

Our senses tired
and turning toward sleep,
our thoughts disordered
and lapped in fur,

your shoulder sleeping
distinct in my hand,
the tally of our remaining encounters
reduced by one.

*

Cut and fold it open,
the thick orange, honey-coarse.
First blood: a saturated essence
tasted between the teeth.

I held the kettle out high
and emptied it
with a shrivelled hiss
boiling into the scalded pot.

A stubborn memory:
her tender, deliberate incursions.

## Morning Coffee

### 1

We thought at first it was a body
rolling up with a blank belly onto the beach
the year our first-born babies died.

A big white earthenware vessel
settled staring up
open mouthed at us.

The first few who reached it
said they thought they caught
a smell of blood and milk.


Soon we were making up stories
about the First People
and telling them to our second born.

*


A loving little boy
        appeared on angel's wings
and showed his empty quiver.
        I filled it out of mine.

He vanished, but remembered:
        every dart
returning furious
        to my heart.

*


At a well beside the way
I alighted and put down
my lips to the water.

You, lifting your face
like a thirsty thing to mine,
I think I know you well:

of character retiring,
settled in your habits,
careful of your appearance;

with eyes open inward;
restless in disposition;
best left alone.

What matter if you seem
assured in your purpose
and animal commitment

but vague in direction
and effect on affairs?
Resolved on perfection

but soon indecisive?
We are all only pilgrims.
Travelling the night.


## 2


It was late. At a side table.
The cup hot in my two hands.
My briefcase against the chair,
with a few drafts debating among themselves.

There were a few of the staff
sitting around the long room.
One or two on each others' minds.

Outside, through the basement window,
the cobbles, opening among the old buildings,
narrowed past the Library
toward the car, still cooling.

A hand at my throat: the shaved leather.
An hour earlier, standing against the sink,
studying the signs. Holding the affected wrist
too long under the scalding tap,
sharp with pain and pleasure…

I pushed the chair back and picked up the notes.
They will be starting to wonder upstairs.
And left my cup
                    for the woman waiting.

# At the Head Table

The air grew dark with anger
toward the close of the celebration.
But remembering his purpose
he kept an even temper

thinking: I have devoted
my life, my entire career,
to the avoidance of affectation,
the way of entertainment

or the specialist response.
With always the same outcome.
Dislike. Misunderstanding.
But I will do what I can.

He rose, adjusting his garments,
lifted the lovely beaker
with the slim amphibian handles,
and turned toward the source of trouble.

'Madam. Your health. Your patience.
Unlock those furious arms,
or we who respect and love you
will have to take offence.

How often, like this evening,
we have sat and watched it happen.
Discussing the same subjects
from our settled points of view,

our cheer turning to bitterness
with one careless word,
and then the loaded silence,
staring straight ahead.

Oh for the simple wisdom
to learn by our experience!
I know from my daily labour
it is not too much to ask.

This lovely cup before us
– this piece before all others –
gave me the greatest trouble,
in impulse and idea

and management of material,
in all the fine requirements
that bring the craftsman's stoop.
Yet proved the most rewarding.

Perfect for its purpose,
holding an ample portion
measured most exactly,
pouring precise and full.

A fit vessel also
for vital decoration.
These marks of waves and footsteps
somewhere by the sea

– in fact a web of order,
each mark accommodating
the shapes of all the others
with none at fault, or false;

a system of live images
making increased response
to each increased demand
in the eye of the beholder,

with a final full response
over the whole surface
– a total theme – presented
to a full intense regard:


Nine waves out, a ship
lying low in the water,
battered from a journey,
the waves lapping around it

marked with the faint detail
of all the perils past.
A few firm footprints
emerging from the ocean

and planted on the seashore;
the sand grains shifted,
marked with the faint detail
of perils still to come.

Nine steps inland
where the two worlds meet, or divide,
a well of pure water,
with the first prints fading.'


He poured her a long portion
of the best blood brandy,
and lifted the brimming beaker
to her motherly regard.

'Remembering the Father,
His insult when offended,
our proneness to offend,
we will drink to His absent shade.'

A smile, dry and lipless
disturbed her stern features.
Her lean arms opened
acknowledging her son.


He limped off leftward
topping up their glasses
along the head table,

and danced off downward
out among the others,
everyone in turn.

from

# The Familiar

(1999)

## I

I was on my own, fumbling at the neglect
in my cell, up under the roof
over Baggot Street. Remembering
our last furious farewell
– face to face, studying each other
with a hardness like hate.
Mismatched, under the sign of sickness.

My last thoughts alone.
Her knock at the door:
her face bold on the landing.
'I brought you a present.'

I lifted in her case.
It was light, but I could tell
she was going to stay.

## III

Muse on my mattress
    with eyes bare
combing her fingers
    down through my hair

Her things on the floor
    a sigh of disorder
box of her body
    in an oxtail odour

Bending above me
    with busy neck
and loose locks
    my mind black


## V

I rose with need in the small hours
and felt my way along the landing
to empty my system beside the sink.

The moon bright
on the three graces above the tank.
The youngest, chosen; stripped and ready.
Her older sister nude behind her,
settling her hair. Their matron mother
to one side, holding the mirror.

I felt my way back afterwards
along the landing, into my place.
Our legs locked in friendship.

from

# Godhead

(1999)

## High Tide: Amagansett

The ocean swell mounted, approaching the land;
folded in a long crest, whitening along its length;
and dismantled in thunder up the miles of shore,

the spent uproar delivering its remains
into the remains of the last wave returning against it
to the sea, into the throat of an overhanging wave.

The waves are alive, arguing among themselves,
hurrying in disorder between two stillnesses:

out beyond the first stir of unrest
at a depth without light;

and in the last lap of salt water stopped at my foot,
discovering the first thought of withdrawal.

# from *Godhead*

## Trinity

The Father
in absolute beauty, absolutely still.
He has done everything in His power.

The Son hanging on high,
reconciling the Father's requirements
with His capacity.

The Third Person
holding Its breath.

from

# Citizen of the World

(2000)

## The Design

Goodness is required.
It is part of the design.
Badness is understood.
It is a lapse, and part of the design.

Acknowledgement of the good
and condemnation of the bad
are required. Lapses
are not understood.

## Complaint

The times were bad
and we were in bad hands.
There was nothing to be done,
only record.

# Echo

Thou shalt not entertain,
    charm or impress;
consider the response
    or the work of others;
confirm viewpoints,
    satisfy expectations,
leave crucial issues confused,
    or impose order.


# Migrants

A pair of living things,
frail, with wings folded up,
are resting on a leaf,
looking in all directions.

They have worked in base impulses,
apart, up out of the earth.
Laboured in change, feeding on their own fat.
And met, resting on their first flight.

Voluptas: stinging and sweet,
starting to die already, exposed to the air.
Vulgaris: restless and sullen.
Lasting a little longer.

Migrants. Of limited distribution.

# *Undine*

Her body bare, her tail
lapped in water off her sea rock,

she has brought her needs to bear
for an hour in the upper air,

calling after the merchantmen
passing on their sea lanes and sky lanes

at the edge of hearing,
their waste widening behind them

(shades at the places of arrival
preparing for their reception;

shades at the places of departure
dispersed, paid in part):


'... Is there anybody passing in command
who will alter course in reply?

Come closer, out toward the edge,
with the others who have turned aside

in answer to my stone song...'
                      (the song fading)

'...and we will dispute together
the detail and the whole...'


Womanbody,
I will be passing closer on the return.

from

# *Littlebody*

(2000)

## *Shop Shut*

I pulled the heavy door over
and leaned my head against it,
    the long key coarse in my face.

Inserted the iron teeth in the box lock
and turned the heart of the handle
    on my den of images. Shop shut.


Summer night, Percy Lane.
The last light full of midges.
    Gnats out of nothing.

# from *Glenmacnass*

## I

I have known the hissing assemblies.
The preference for the ease of the spurious
– the measured poses and stupidities.

On a fragrant slope descending into the smoke
over our foul ascending city
I turned away in refusal,
holding a handful of high grass
sweet and grey to my face.

## V

I left the road where a stile entered the quiet wood.
Dry trees standing in order in their own grain.

Close up, on a patch of bark, a mouse body.
Upside down. Wings flat.

Meant only to be half seen
quick in the half light: little leather angel
falling everywhere, snapping at the invisible.

## VI Littlebody

Up on the high road, as far as the sheepfold
into the wind, and back. The sides of the black bog channels
dug down in the water. The white cottonheads
on the old cuttings nodding everywhere.
Around one more bend, toward the car shining in the distance.

From a stony slope half way, behind a rock prow
with the stones on top for an old mark,
the music of pipes, distant and clear.

I was climbing up, making no noise
and getting close, when the music stopped,
leaving a pagan shape in the air.


There was a hard inhale,
a base growl,
and it started again, in a guttural dance.

I looked around the edge
– and it was Littlebody. Hugging his bag
under his left arm, with his eyes closed.

I slipped. Our eyes met.
He started scuttling up the slope with his gear
and his hump, elbows out and neck back.

But I shouted:
                'Stop, Littlebody!
I found you fair and I want my due.'

He stopped and dropped his pipes,
and spread his arms out, waiting for the next move.
I heard myself reciting:

'Demon dwarf
with the German jaw,
surrender your purse
with the ghostly gold.'

He took out a fat purse,
put it down on a stone
and recited in reply, in a voice too big for his body:

'You found me fair,
and I grant your wishes.
But we'll meet again,
when I dance in your ashes.'

He settled himself down once more
and bent over the bag,
                              looking off to one side.


'I thought I was safe up here.
You have to give the music a while to itself sometimes,
up out of the huckstering

– jumping around in your green top hat
and showing your skills
with your eye on your income.'


He ran his fingers up and down the stops,
then gave the bag a last squeeze.
His face went solemn,

his fingertips fondled all the right places,
and he started a slow air
                              out across the valley.

                    *

I left him to himself.
And left the purse where it was.
I have all I need for the while I have left

without taking unnecessary risks.
And made my way down to the main road
with my mind on our next meeting.


*from* LITTLEBODY (2000)                          167

from

# *Marginal Economy*

(2006)

## *Marcus Aurelius*

### I On the Ego

Gaspbegotten. In shockfuss.
Out of nowhere.

Bent in blind sleep
  over a closed book.


Through the red neck
  cast out,

his first witness
  the gasp of loss,

to lie spent a while
  in the bloodstained shallows.


A little flesh. A little breath.
  And the mind governing.

## II

Affairs were troubled in those days,
with over-confidence and ignorance everywhere.
A citizen, absent a while on an undertaking,
would find only increased coarseness on his return.

He himself, notable in his time and place,
and a major figure as later times would agree
(though for reasons that would have surprised
                                        his fellow citizens)
was in a false position :

                        cast in a main role,
while fitted with the instincts of an observer;
contending throughout his life with violent forces
that were to him mainly irrelevant.

Threatened on the Northern border by brutal tribes
with no settled homes – swift in the attack,
inspiring great fear; but ignorant and unskilled,
swift equally in the retreat –

these he dealt with, stemming their advance
and scattering them among their own confusions.
It was after his death that they resumed their incursions
that led to the break-up of the Western Empire.

A vaguer-seeming contagion out of the East,
more deadly in the longer term – in the citizens'
depths of will, and their dealings among themselves –
this he neglected.

                        Though it seems in retrospect
that nothing of any substance could have been done.
That it was irresistible
and in the movement and nature of things.

Called upon for decisive positive action,
at which he was more than averagely effective;
but preferring to spend his time in abstract inquiry,
for which he was essentially ungifted;

he kept a private journal, in Greek, for which
he is best remembered. Almost certainly
because it engaged so much of the baffled humane
in him, in his Imperial predicament:

accepting established notions of a cosmos
created and governed by a divine intelligence
– while not believing in an afterlife;

proposing exacting moral goals, with man
an element in that divine intelligence
– while pausing frequently to contemplate

the transient brutishness of earthly life,
our best experience of which concludes
with death, unaccountable and blank.

As to the early Christians, who might have helped
with their new simplicities, he took no interest,
unsystematic in their persecution,
permitting the martyrdoms to run their course.


### III

Faustina, wife of Marcus, developed a passion
for a certain gladiator. She confessed this
to her husband, who had the gladiator killed
and his wife bathed in the blood. They lay together,
· and she conceived and brought into the world
the son Commodus, who grew to rule
with Marcus for a while as Emperor,
and became sole ruler on Marcus' death
– coming to terms quickly with the Northern tribes.

His rule was arbitrary, bloody-minded,
centred on the Games; and culminated
in the belief that he was Hercules.
His plan to appear for an Imperial function
in the arena, dressed as a gladiator,
led to public outcry, and his assassination,

strangled in private among his close advisers.
His death, succeeded by chaos and civil war,
ended one of the Empire's longest periods
of civic affluence and stability.

## *Blood of the Innocent*

### I

From the day she was discovered
we watched over her and gave in to her,
and let her have everything.

But kept her to herself.
She grew lonely and sunk in on herself,
yawning in everybody's face.

*

We are gathered in rows
   on the steep steps,
a single being
   breathing together.

With apron stiff
   and jewelled beard
he stands at the block
   in the place of praise.

## II

The last time in anybody's memory
there was anything like this up here
was when that young local genius
tried to get them to change the system,

persuading the Authorities
that making an offering back to the source
with an act of thanks
is an interruption of the process.


That the life-form as we have it
is inadequate in itself; but that
having discovered the compensatory devices

of Love and the creative and religious imaginations
we should gather in each generation
all the good we can from the past,

add our own best and,
advancing in our turn
                              outward into the dark,

leave to those behind us,
with Acts of Hope and Encouragement,
a growing total of Good (adequately recorded),

the Arts and the Sciences,
with their abstractions and techniques
– all of human endeavour –

in a flexible and elaborating
time-resisting fabric
of practical and moral beauty…


\*

Meek and mild,
with body marked,
our dear daughter
steps forward.


## Songs of Understanding

### I

A major element of waste
    needed in the living process,
with an element of excess
    in the constituent materials;
distinguishing basic features
    performing no apparent function,
and playing no discernible part
    in countering any negative forces,
but which are nonetheless clearly essential
    for fulfilment of the process,
and which, if removed, would establish
    an emptiness under the heart.

I feel these, and allow my arms
    to fall open in resignation,
desiring an understanding.

## II

Accepting the waste and the excess,
    and a fundamental inadequacy
in the structure as a whole
    and in each individual part,
there is still an ongoing dynamic
    in the parts as they succeed each other,
and in the assembling record,
    that registers as positive.

This can be thought of as purposeful,
    permitting the illusion,
to a self-selected few,
    of the positive participation
in a communal endeavour
    with a final meaningful goal
– imprecisely defined,
    subject to continual change
and calling for constant effort,
    but sufficient to give the feeling
of advancement toward an End.

## III

Reclaiming out of the past
    all the good you can use,
add all the good that you can
    and offer it all onward.

## IV

Through a fault on the outermost rim
    left open for the length of a lifetime
a glimpse of preoccupied purpose
    chilled the blood in my face.

# Note on Peppercanister Poems

Peppercanister was established in 1972 as a small publishing enterprise, with the purpose of issuing occasional special items from our home in Dublin, across the Grand Canal from St Stephen's Church, known locally as 'The Peppercanister'.

*A Selected Life*, published in July 1972, is a funeral poem written in memory of Seán Ó Riada, composer and musician, who died in October 1971. *Vertical Man* was published in August 1973 as a sequel to *A Selected Life*; it is set in Philadelphia on the first anniversary of Ó Riada's death.

Peppercanister editions have continued as a form of draft publication; distributed currently by Dedalus Press, Dublin; Carcanet Press in the United Kingdom; and Dufour Editions in the United States and Canada. Collections are issued occasionally in book form: *Fifteen Dead* published by Dolmen Press in 1976; *One and Other Poems* by the Dolmen Press and Oxford University Press in 1979; *Peppercanister Poems (1972-1978)* by Wake Forest University Press in 1979 in the United States; *Blood and Family* (1988) and *From Centre City* (1994) by Oxford University Press. Full collections, complete to the time of publication, are included in *Collected Poems* (2001, Carcanet Press), and most recently in *Collected Poems* (2006, Wake Forest University Press).

# Index of First Lines

# Index of Titles